EDINBURGH

Scotland's Capital

with many original photographs by
Alan Daiches, John Dewar, Duncan Dingsdale,
A. F. Kersting, A. D. S. Macpherson,
Eric de Maré, John Porteous, Paul Shillabeer,
and others

*The Old Fountain Well in
the High Street*

EDINBURGH

OLIVER & BOYD

EDINBURGH

EDINBURGH – SCOTLAND'S CAPITAL

1. *The crown of St Giles.*

SCOTLAND'S CAPITAL

OLIVER & BOYD LTD

Tweeddale Court
Edinburgh 1

39A Welbeck Street
London W1

First published 1967

Designed by Ruari McLean

Printed in Great Britain
by Pillans & Wilson Ltd
Edinburgh

2 (overleaf). *The new University Buildings round George Square,
the McEwan Hall, the Castle, St. John's Tolbooth, the Old College,
St. Giles, the Radical Road, Salisbury Crags, and Hutton's Section, from the Hawse.*

ACKNOWLEDGMENTS

In expressing our gratitude for all the help that many of our fellow citizens have given us in compiling this book, my colleagues and I wish especially to thank: the Right Hon. Lord Clyde, Lord Justice General; Mr Charles Stewart, Secretary of Edinburgh University; Miss Lorna R. Rhind, Publicity Officer of the City of Edinburgh; and Mrs Norma Armstrong, of the Edinburgh Room, Edinburgh Public Library.

On behalf of the publishers, we wish also to thank the following for granting permission to reproduce the illustrations listed after their names: Lord Clyde, 28, and, with Mr T. W. Strachan, Clerk of the Faculty of Advocates, 29; Mr J. B. I. McTavish, Queen's and Lord Treasurer's Remembrancer, 17; Mr P. J. Oliphant, Deputy Keeper of the Signet, and the Council of the Society of Writers to the Signet, 58; the Lord Provost, Magistrates, and Council of Edinburgh, 25, 26, 27; Mr C. S. Minto, City Librarian and Curator, Edinburgh Public Libraries, endpapers, 81, 82, 138; the Trustees of the British Museum, 12-13, 136; Mr Charles Stewart, 59, 61, and, with Prof. D. Abercrombie, 57; the Rev. Dr H. C. Whitley, Minister of St Giles, 21; and Mr Charles Ballantyne, Secretary of the New Club, Edinburgh, 137. We are also grateful to all the photographers and owners of copyrights whose names are mentioned in the *Notes on Several of the Illustrations* or in the *List of Original Photographs* both printed on the last page of the book; and for permission to reprint three of the poems included in the Anthology, we wish to make grateful acknowledgment to Sig. Eugenio Montale and Arnaldo Mondadori ('Vento Sulla Mezzaluna'), Mr Robert Garioch ('Embro tae the Ploy' and 'Vox Populi'), and Mr Sydney Goodsir Smith ('Auld Reekie 1963').

Finally I wish to express my own personal gratitude to Mrs Janet Rae, Miss Jean Ann Anderson, Mr Moray McLaren, and Mr R. G. Sutherland for all the hard work that they have done for me, and for all that they have each contributed to the book.

R. L. C. LORIMER

12 September 1966

3. *A late medieval carving of the City's arms in St Giles.*

CONTENTS

4. *George Street, the Calton Hill, Princes Street and its Gardens, the Castle, the Royal Mile, Salisbury Crags, and Arthur's Seat, with Portobello, Musselburgh, and the Firth of Forth in the background.*

INTRODUCTION

Edinburgh is a city of hills. This is the fundamental fact that dictated its medieval shape and gave its Georgian town-planning a character all its own. It is a city abounding in natural drama, with many rock cliffs, ridges, banks, and braes, which at every turn enliven the perspective and give the architecture an exciting emphasis.

A few years ago, the Cockburn Association set out to compile a list of the city's most prized views. The intention was to identify those vistas which citizens should most jealously guard. The catalogue ran to an astounding length and owed part of its extent to Edinburgh's ubiquitous hills. The response emphasised the keen interest that Edinburgh folk take in the beauty and preservation of their environment.

One of the most spectacular views of the city is from the Castle, on a day when the sun is sparkling on the Firth of Forth. In the centre of this magnificent prospect the city lies cradled between hills and sea. Behind the spectator, southwards, it rolls away till it laps the foot of the Pentland Hills on the horizon. It is one city, and yet the spectator high on the Castle Rock is looking at many communities, each with its distinct and contrasting characteristics, social or architectural. Cramond, Portobello, Morningside, Trinity, Stockbridge, Marchmont, Grange, Sciennes, Newington, Gilmerton, Granton, Liberton, Oxgangs, Corstorphine. . . . No matter how often the beholder scans this extensive skyline, his gaze always, in the end, reverts to the city centre, and receives an immediate impression of contrast between the medieval Old Town set on the Castle ridge, and the neo-Georgian New Town across the valley to the north—one the seat of violent history and tradition: the other a carefully planned monument to an era of elegance and grace. The demarcation between old and new is easily recognised, especially by the spectator on the Castle summit. It is Princes Street Gardens, once the site of the old Nor' Loch.

It is not easy to pinpoint, with any accuracy, the moment at which Edinburgh emerged as capital of Scotland. James II (1437-60) began holding his Parliaments in the town, which still huddled on the ridge to the east of the Castle. Until James VI ascended the English throne at the Union of the Crowns in 1603, Scottish monarchs regarded Edinburgh as their seat of government and law. Even after the Union of Parliaments in 1707, and the removal of the government to London, Edinburgh continued to be Scotland's legal centre. It also continued as the administrative centre for the Church of Scotland. Intellectually, Edinburgh experienced its golden age in the eighteenth and nineteenth centuries, when men like David Hume, Adam Smith, and Walter Scott gave the city an international reputation. The scientific achievements of James Young Simpson, Joseph Lister, and Alexander Graham Bell also brought renown. All this, it might be argued, sprang from the decision to create the New Town. In draining the Nor' Loch and leaping the valley, the citizens of Edinburgh sought spaciousness and found an intellectual grandeur. It is perhaps significant that, in the plans of young James Craig, Queen Street, with its view of the Forth, was considered the desirable quarter—not Princes Street, with its view towards the Castle, which was the symbol of the old. The plea made by Lord Provost George Drummond to his fellow citizens to leave the cramped but traditionally safe Castle ridge for the airy spaces of the New Town was the beginning of a great adventure. It symbolised a clean break with tradition, and the birth of a creative spirit which has continued to this day.

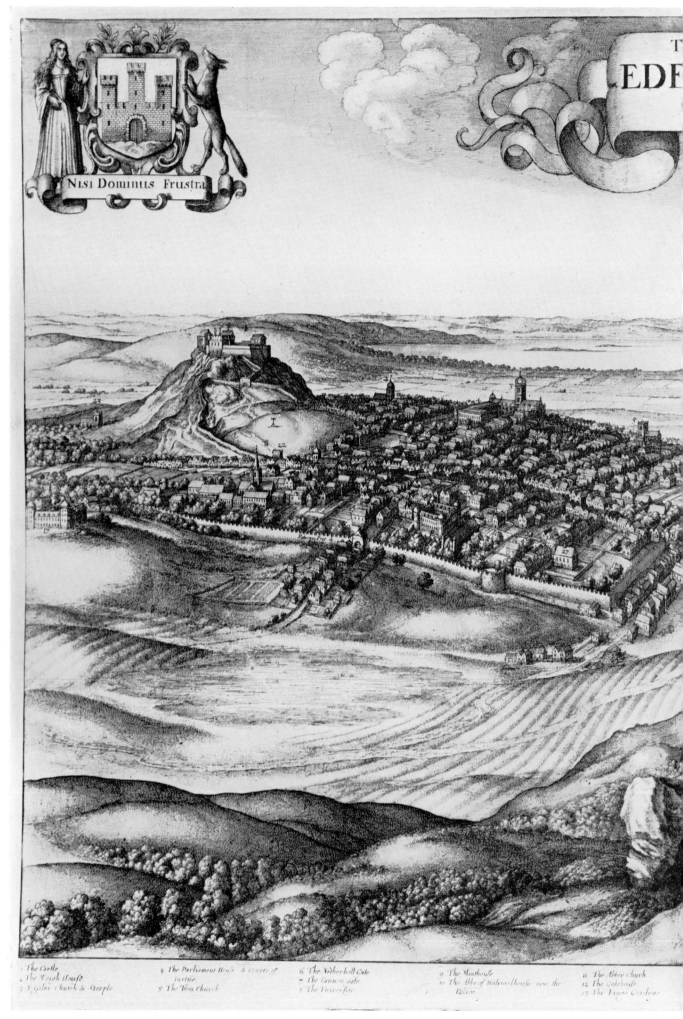

The coat of arms bears the motto: **NISI DOMINUS FRUSTRA**

Banner text: **T** / **EDE**

Key (partially legible):
- 1. The Castle
- 2. The Weigh House
- 3. S. Giles Church & Steeple
- 4. The Parliament House & Courts of Justice
- 5. The Tron Church
- 6. The Netherbow Gate
- 7. The Cannon gate
- 8. The University
- 9. The Minthouse
- 10. The Abbey of Holyroodhouse now the Palace
- 11. The Abbey church
- 12. The Gatehouse
- 13. The Kings Gardens

5. 'The Citie of Edenburgh from the South'.
Etching, in two sheets, 41·0 × 61 cm., by W. Hollar, 1670. British Museum, ref. 70-5-14-253; Parthey, No. 973. A vixen has incorrectly been substituted for a hind as sinister supporter of the City's escutcheon.

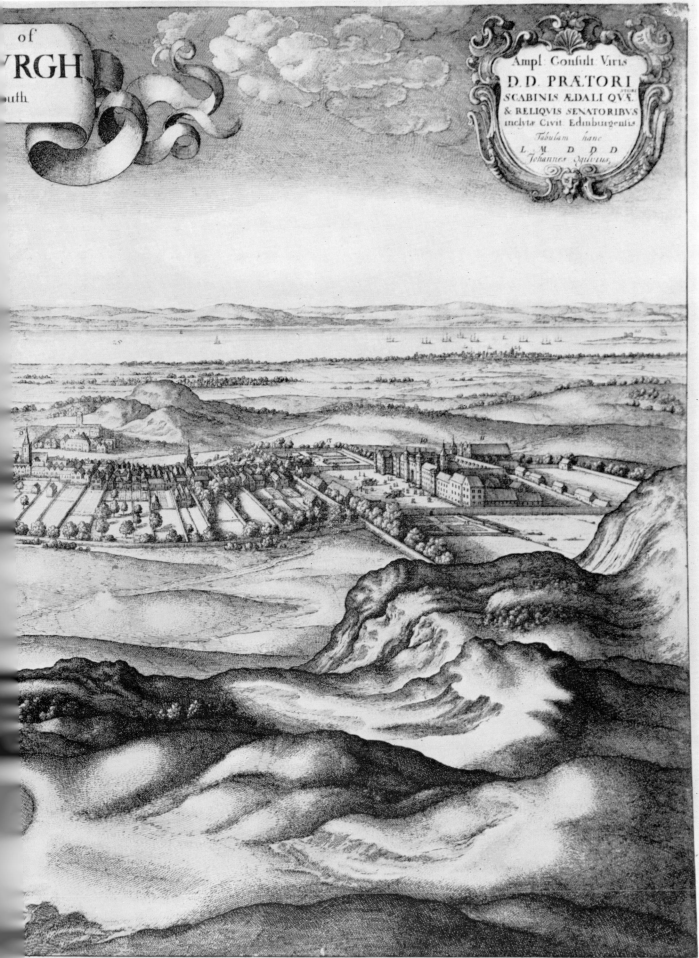

Ampl: Confult Viris
D.D. PRÆTORI
SCABINIS ÆDALI QVÆ
& RELIQVIS SENATORIBVS
inclytæ Civit. Edinburgentis
Tabulam hanc
L.M.D.D.D.
Iohannes Ogilvius.

ourt of the Palace	17 Heriots Hospitall	20 Potewate Port	23 S.ᵗ Cuthberts Church	26 Inchkeith Castle
olledge Church & Hospitall	18 S.ᵗ Magdalene Chappell	21 S.ᵗ Mary Port	24 The Citty of Leith	27 The fire Schole
riers Church	19 Bristo Port	22 West Port	25 The firth of Edinburgh	

I. THE CASTLE

Edinburgh's role as the capital of Scotland developed, in the beginning, from the fact of the Castle Rock.

The Rock, an oval-shaped mass of basalt, 437 feet above sea level, is one of Edinburgh's five extinct volcanoes. Its physical character made it a natural place of defence and, consequently, in the turbulent world of royal politics, a point of power. To the Romans the geographical position also was important, for, as a hill fort, the site commanded the point where the Roman road from the south reached the Forth. In subsequent centuries, the tide of war was to wash over the Rock many times. However, its future as a centre of trade and political influence was assured. Today Edinburgh no longer needs a fortress to maintain its status: but the Castle and Rock remain the City's focal point—its heart and centre.

Most visitors immediately appreciate the physical fact of the Rock—if only because they must look for ways to circumvent it. The streams of modern traffic flowing eastward—either along Princes Street, or up Johnston Terrace immediately under the Rock face—follow the direction of the glacier which, 125,000 years ago, gouged out the valleys and thus isolated the Castle Rock. For indwellers in Edinburgh, the dominance of the Rock, which in fact is not as high as Arthur's Seat, assumes different proportions. Indeed, Edinburgh folk are so accustomed to its presence that even when a haar creeps in from the sea to hide it, they continue to feel its presence. Consciously or unconsciously, good weather or bad, they orientate their movements on it.

The best views of the Castle often come unexpectedly. To see it from King's Stables Road under a full moon is to glimpse a scene not of this century. Or, on a fine day, turn the corner from Rose Street into Castle Street and the scene becomes too much of a theatrical backdrop to seem true. Equally impressive is the view from the Grassmarket in a fog. Then the grey walls seem to lour over one precipitously. From inside the Castle, too, the steepness of this southern cliff becomes overwhelming. To stand in the tiny room where James VI was born and gaze out of the window straight down the Rock face is not for the light-headed.

Looking now at the numerous buildings which populate the Castle Rock, it is difficult to appreciate that this fortification once contained extensive grazing lands. A drawing dated 1647, after Gordon of Rothiemay, shows the Castle itself was still very small indeed, even though the entire Rock had been walled in. The Half-Moon Battery, Royal Lodgings, and Great Hall stand out as the major buildings, with the much weathered St Margaret's Chapel appearing on a lonely outcrop further away. Initially, of course, there were only turf and wooden huts.

In 1296, Edward I used engines to hurl stones through the roofs of buildings inside the walls, and successfully attacked the Castle fortification. Sixteen years later, Sir Thomas Randolph, Earl of Moray, made his well-known climb over the north wall and routed the English. Following the orders of King Robert the Bruce, the Castle, with the exception of St Margaret's Chapel, was rased to the ground.

Gradually the Castle again took shape, becoming, with each successive addition, more invincible. Although battles about it continued, it was never again rased. The last siege occurred in 1689, when for several months the Duke of Gordon held out against the forces of William of Orange.

6. *The Castle, from the south-east.*

One of the remaining symbols of Scotland's stature as an independent Kingdom is the ancient Crown, which, with the Sceptre and Sword of State, comprise the 'Honours of Scotland'.

According to one well-known legend, the Crown contains a circlet of gold with which the Countess of Buchan crowned Bruce at Scone in 1306. But, according to Barbour, Bruce was only enthroned in 1306; and he was not crowned until many years later. In its present form, the Crown probably dates from 1540, when it was remodelled for James V. The bonnet, ermine, and cushion are modern.

The Crown is fashioned in a circle of gold set with 22 large gems and 20 pearls, at least seven of which come from Scotland—a likely source being the lower reaches of the River Tay. The four golden arches are ornamented with gold and red enamelled oak leaves, believed to be of French workmanship. A globe of blue enamelled gold, signifying sovereign authority, sits at the juncture of the gold arches. This is surmounted by a large cross in gold and black enamel, set with an amethyst and Oriental pearls. The gold in the Crown is of Scottish origin and may have been extracted from the mines at Crawford Muir.

The Sceptre, a long hexagonal rod, with a head and a globe surmounted by a finial, was presented by Pope Alexander VI to James IV in 1494. It was altered and almost entirely remade in 1536 for James V. The head of the Sceptre carries the figures of the Virgin and Child, St James and St Andrew. The globe is of rock crystal and the silver finial is surmounted by a large Scottish pearl. Pope Julius II presented the Sword of State to James IV in 1507. The blade carries the Pope's legend, and figures believed to represent Sts Peter and Paul.

In 1651, when the Cromwellian forces were penetrating into Scotland, the Honours were removed, for safety, to Dunnottar Castle, near Stonehaven. The Castle, a cliff stronghold surrounded on three sides by water, had a meagre garrison of forty men under Sir George Ogilvie of Barras.

For months, Dunnottar Castle was besieged by Parliamentary forces under General Overton; and, on the verge of starvation, Ogilvie was forced to surrender. On entering the Castle, however, the English found the Crown and Regalia gone.

What is believed to have happened is this. Mrs Granger, wife of the minister of the neighbouring parish of Kinneff, went to the Castle to visit the Governor's wife, taking with her a maid carrying a distaff and bundle of flax. When she left the Castle, Mrs Granger, the Crown hid beneath her skirts, was gallantly helped to her horse by an English general. Her maid carried the Sceptre and Sword, in place of the distaff. The Regalia were then hidden beneath the floor of the kirk at Kinneff, until the Restoration in 1660, when they were returned to Edinburgh Castle. The Governor's wife, who allegedly devised the conspiracy, was put in prison with her husband, where she later died.

When the Scottish and English Acts of Union were passed in 1707, the Honours of Scotland were delivered to the Commissioners of the Treasury, who locked them in an oak chest and forgot about them. In 1817 Sir Walter Scott persuaded the Prince Regent to grant a warrant for a search to be made for the Scottish Regalia. They were discovered during an emotional occasion, at which Scott was present, in what we now know as the Crown Room. After more than a hundred years of concealment, the Honours were unchanged—only tarnished and soiled with dust. They were restored to the people on 4 February 1818; and since then have retained their place of veneration in the Crown Room.

16

7. *The Crown of Scotland.*

9. *Tolbooth St John's, St Giles, Salisbury Crags, and Arthur's Seat, from the Castle.*

The Castle Rock is not reduced from the air. Rather, it assumes a different aspect than when viewed from the ground. The Esplanade, so often filled with touring buses, has a unique connexion with Nova Scotia. During the reign of Charles I (1625-49), permission was granted to the Earl of Stirling to colonise Nova Scotia and to sell baronetcies to prospective settlers. To enable the new baronets to take sasine (the receipt of a token amount of soil by which the transaction was regarded as legally completed) a royal mandate was granted converting part of Castle Hill into Nova Scotian territory. The spot is believed to lie just east of the drawbridge.

Nowadays, the Esplanade provides a historic setting for the Edinburgh Festival Tattoo.

Distant yet overpowering stands Arthur's Seat. Dictionaries refuse to define 'mountain' in terms of height. In their tour of the Hebrides in 1773, Boswell described one of the mountains in Kintail (probably Faochaig) as 'immense', but Dr Johnson retorted 'No, it is no more than a considerable protuberance'. Edinburgh people are proud of *their* protuberance—it is indeed considerable!

19

10. *Mons Meg, with visitors. On the horizon both Forth Bridges can be seen.*

Every year almost half a million visitors and Edinburgh people alike climb up to the Forewall Battery of the Castle. It is a spectacular vantage point from which to see first Princes Street and the Gardens, and then the New Town, marching down to the Firth of Forth.

A familiar sentinel here is Mons Meg, a fifteenth-century iron bombard once affectionately called 'Muckle [big] Meg'. If loaded with iron shot she had a range of 1,500 yards; if loaded with stone, the range increased to 2,900 yards. She herself weighs five tons.

Meg, a startling contrast to the Castle's more modern artillery, has a doubtful origin. She has been credited to Mons, either in Flanders or in Galloway in the south west of Scotland: but popular tradition holds that Meg was forged within the Castle by Robert Borthwick, gunner to James IV (1488-1513). In 1759, Meg was removed to the Tower of London, and there she remained until 1829, when (mainly in deference to the representations of Sir Walter Scott) she was returned to the Castle with full military honours.

Near Mons Meg is the oldest building in Edinburgh, St Margaret's Chapel. Dating from the eleventh century, the chapel is named after the Saxon wife of King Malcolm Canmore (1058-93). At one time, after the Cromwellian siege, the chapel was used as a magazine.

20

11. *Princes Street Gardens, the New Town, the Firth of Forth, the coast of Fife, and the Lomonds, from the Castle.*

On being confronted with the view from the Castle Hill, Dr Johnson said 'The noblest prospect which a Scotchman ever sees, is the high road that leads him to London'. There are many nobler prospects in Scotland facing north, with the spectator's back to England. Among these is the view of Princes Street from the Castle battlements. It is that thoroughfare with which visitors are most familiar. Wherever else they may have been in their Edinburgh perambulations, they cannot have missed Princes Street.

Architecturally, the street is a hotchpotch of styles prevalent, at various times, during the past two hundred years. Some of the more recent shops stand out because of their simplicity of modern design. On closer inspection, however, one can still pick out the earlier architectural oddities—turrets and towers, gables and ironwork, dormer windows, and curious roof-top rotundas.

The northward prospect from the Castle also takes in the Ross Bandstand and West Princes Street Gardens. The Gardens, when originally laid out, were meant to be private; and those who sought to use their expanse, for a promenade, had to pay for their keys. Nor were smoking and Bath chairs allowed! Nowadays the Gardens welcome all members of the public who come to see the Floral Clock, to sit in the sunshine, or, on a summer's evening, to enjoy performances of Scottish country dancing and folk singing or piping in the Ross Bandstand.

21

12. *Wallace, with one of the Scots for whom he bled.*

Sculptures of two of Scotland's heroes, Sir William Wallace, by Alexander Carrick, and King Robert the Bruce, by T. J. Clapperton, guard the ditch-protected entrance to the Castle. Wallace, the people's hero, was particularly noted for his guerilla warfare against Edward I. Edward later captured Wallace and had him put to death, as a 'traitor', in 1305. King Robert finally defeated Edward II at Bannockburn, near Stirling, in 1314.

With its ample gardens, wide streets, squares, and places, and many long vistas, Edinburgh is pre-eminently a spacious city. But this was not always so; and the Old Town is riddled with wynds or narrow lanes and passages starkly in contrast with the lofty and generous spaciousness of Edinburgh, old and new.

In the *Shorter Oxford English Dictionary*, 'wynd' is defined as an 'alley in a Scotch town'. Probably, however, it is in fact the Scottish spelling of the English word 'wind', and means no more than that these ancient architectural paths were irregular in their course.

Perhaps the most spectacular wynds are the ones on the north side of the Lawnmarket and High Street, which dipped down towards the banks of the Nor' Loch. Now, from the heights of the Old Town, they give all who pass by frequent dramatic glimpses of the Forth, and also of Fife. In these Royal Mile wynds there are still occasional twisting staircases with a left-hand spiral, designed to favour the defending swordsman. Collectors of historical data can also find numerous 'marriage-lintels' and other doorway stones with religious inscriptions and dates which the passage of time has made barely recognisable. The carved initials in the marriage-lintels are those of the husband and wife, perhaps newly married, who set up home there.

One of the more pleasing wynds, away from the Royal Mile, is a steep and perilous lane, with many steps, which stretches from the east end of the Castle Esplanade by way of Johnston Terrace, to the once joyful, yet ill-omened, Grassmarket, where festivals were held and public executions took place.

The Grassmarket is a wide, historic square on the verge of the Old Town. It is generally approached by King's Stables Road, the curving slope of Victoria Street, Candlemaker Row, or the West Port. Grain and cattle markets were held here weekly until 1911, when they were removed to Saughton. Here one can see the old White Hart Inn, patronised by Burns and Wordsworth; and, at the eastern end, the tracing of a cross of rose-coloured cobblestones in the roadway where more than a hundred Covenanters died, rather than abandon their religious beliefs. Most of the famous Grassmarket landmarks have now disappeared, including the Greyfriars' Monastery, which once stood near the south-east corner. Gone too is Tanner's Close, which was situated near the West Port [gate] near Lady Lawson Street. In this close lived the infamous murderers Burke and Hare, who sold their victims' bodies for medical dissection. The exact number of victims was never known, but one luckless lad who fell into their pitiless clutches was 'Daft Jamie', a well-known Edinburgh character and a popular figure, whose death incensed public opinion against the accused.

The old roaring, rambling crowd of citizens who used to tumble down the Castle Wynd on their way to the Grassmarket, have disappeared. There are not many today who will tolerate its steepness. It has been superseded by easier-travelled routes. However, one sometimes sees an occasional passer-by still making use of one of Edinburgh's most notable antiquities.

22

13. *Trysted: in the Grassmarket, at the foot of the Castle Wynd.*

14. *Tolbooth St John's, Ramsay Garden, St Giles, and New College, from the Castle.*

From Princes Street the most distinctive route to the heart of the Royal Mile is the Mound, an artificial causeway created from two million cartloads of soil excavated during construction of the New Town. According to tradition, a Lawnmarket clothier was the first to dump stones and rubbish across the swamp of the Nor' Loch, and for some years this crude causeway was called 'Geordie Boyd's Mud Brig' in his honour. In 1781 Boyd's short-cut to the New Town and his customers was officially sanctioned by the Town Council, who ordered that all earth taken from the foundations of new buildings should be dumped opposite Hanover Street. It is estimated that at one time 1,800 cartloads were laid daily.

Near the top of the Mound stands the New College of the Church of Scotland, designed by William Henry Playfair (1789-1857) in 1846. Beside it is the Assembly Hall, meeting-place of the annual General Assembly of the Church.

The Royal Scottish Academy and National Gallery of Scotland, at the foot of the Mound, were both designed by Playfair.

For many years these fine buildings were deeply discoloured by smoke from the railway, but with the almost total disappearance of steam engines from this route measures were taken to clean both buildings. Thus they regained the brightness, near-white or soft ochre, which enhances their appearance in so many of the nineteenth-century prints made before the railway rudely thrust itself into Princes Street gardens.

The National Gallery contains a small but splendid collection of French, Dutch, and Italian masterpieces. Scottish painters are, of course, well represented, including two of Edinburgh's own—Allan Ramsay (1713-84) and Sir Henry Raeburn (1756-1823). A wide selection of Raeburn's best-known portraits of eminent Scotsmen is on view, as well as one of Ramsay's most delightful paintings, *The Painter's Wife*.

This view of the Mound gives some impression of the width of that artificial thoroughfare and also of its classic nature. It is hard to believe now that Lord Cockburn, the respected chronicler of his time, once called the Mound 'that abominable encumbrance' and that Sir Walter Scott described it as 'that huge deformity'. The massive outline which the great men found offensive so long ago has been softened and mellowed by the passage of time, by the growth of the trees along its flanks, and by landscaped green spaces tended by the City's gardeners.

15. *Princes Street, the Royal Scottish Academy, and the National Gallery, from Ramsay Lane.*

To visitors, Edinburgh initially appears to be all uphill. Apart from the level expanse of Princes Street, it seems to be a complex of gradients, hills, and steps.

The steps, of course, are handy short-cuts, and time has not lessened their value. Edinburgh people use them with respect for their physical demands, and for their historic and scenic associations. Stand at the top of the steps leading up past the National Gallery and watch the slow progression of pedestrians inching up the hill. You will soon learn that a slow climb is most advantageous to the lungs —it is the infrequent users of steps who arrive at the top quickly, but breathlessly. Or inspect some of the closes on the north side of the High Street and you will find steps which seem to break off in mid-air, with only a cameo of the New Town beyond them.

The steps of Castle Wynd, leading up from the Grassmarket to Castle Hill, are unique in their way. Those who make the climb on a summer's evening may find the colourful spectacle of the marching pipes and drums of the Scottish Horse or the Argyll and Sutherland Highlanders beating Retreat on the Castle Esplanade. If not, there is still ample reward at the top of the steps, because the Castle Hill has many historic associations.

One of the few remaining original buildings on Castle Hill, and the first to come into view at the top of the steps, is Cannonball House. This four-storey tenement dates from the time of Charles I (1625-49) and, although in direct line of approaching armies, has withstood three sieges of the Castle. The cannonball lodged in the gable-end of the house was allegedly fired from the Half-Moon Battery at the Highlanders who occupied the town during the Jacobite Rebellion of 1745. A more prosaic explanation, however, is that it was deliberately fixed in the wall to mark the high water level at Comiston Reservoir.

Across the street from Cannonball House is Ramsay Garden, the original part of which was built by Allan Ramsay, the poet, in 1743. Viewed from the Princes Street side, the original villa is octagonal in shape. Ramsay's son, the painter, enlarged the original villa and raised the larger buildings to the east.

At the beginning of the eighteenth century, the Castle Hill was a favourite promenade for local citizenry. Indeed, in 1709, the Town Council was moved to comment that the Lord's Day was being 'profaned by people standing in the streets and vaguing [wandering] to fields, gardens and the Castle Hill'. One of the grislier reasons for its popularity was its use for executions for treason, heresy, and sorcery. A bronze well called the Witches' Fountain, at the north-east corner of the Castle Esplanade, commemorates the site of these unhappy events. Carved on the well are some of the symbols associated with witchcraft—a serpent representing the god of medicine, the face of the goddess of health, and the evil eye.

Between 1479 and 1722, about 300 witches are said to have been 'worrit at ane stake and brunt'—that is, tied to a stake, strangled, and burnt. In 1659 when five women were burnt at the stake at the same time, one of the many charges against them was that they had 'danced with the devill'.

One of the most unhappy executions was that of the beautiful Lady Jane Douglas, widow of John, Lord Glamis, who was accused by a rejected suitor of trying to kill the King by poison and sorcery. If the charge of sorcery had not been made, she might perhaps have lived. The superstitions of the time convicted her, however, and after being 'examined on the rack' she was burnt at the stake, in view of her son and second husband.

27

16. *Near the top of the Castle Wynd.*

17. *The Castle, from the north east.*

The north face of the Castle Rock, viewed to advantage through the iron railings on the Mound, once dropped directly into the waters of the Nor' Loch. An artificial creation of James II (1437-60), the Loch covered an unseemly marshland and was intended to fortify the defences of the Castle Rock. Eventually it proved, however, to be a weakness; and, although it was useful for ducking witches, and for drowning unwanted cats and dogs, it was also a favourite route for smuggling spirits and other contraband into the burgh.

Viewed from the north-east, the Rock still seems just as impregnable as when, early in 1314, Randolph, Earl of Moray, scaled the walls and captured the Castle, in Bruce's cause. The north face of the Castle Rock has been the scene of climbing in a more sporting vein. On this side are the projecting pieces of rock called the 'Kittle[tricky] Nine-Steps'. In a footnote in *Redgauntlet*, Sir Walter Scott described this passage as 'a pass on the very brink of the Castle Rock . . . , by which it is just possible for a goat, or high school boy, to turn the corner of the building where it rises from the edge of the precipice'.

One of Edinburgh's most notable characteristics is its spaciousness.

For the half million dwellers who occupy the city's 34,781 acres, the parks and other open spaces are a welcome premium. Some of the credit for this feature is due to the natural forces which pushed up Arthur's Seat and Blackford Hill and laid the loch at Duddingston. But man was responsible for some of the amplitude, and in the New Town made certain that the airy atmosphere was continued. The most famous of the City's public gardens are, of course, those that lie in the large dip of land between Princes Street and the Castle and Old Town.

From the southern side of these gardens, particularly in summer, the trees and rolling turf provide a luxuriant frame for the classic art galleries of the Mound and other familiar landmarks. Rising over the roof of the National Gallery is the Gothic spire of the Scott Monument, said to be the world's largest memorial to a man of letters. It was designed by Sir George Meikle Kemp and completed in 1844. A climb up the 287 steps of the Monument is apt to take one's breath, but the view from the top is rewarding. Here one glimpses a different aspect of Edinburgh. From the top the city seems everywhere present and all-embracing.

18. *The Royal Scottish Academy, National Gallery, and Scott Monument, from West Princes Street Gardens.*

19. *The Lawnmarket, St Giles, and the Tron Kirk, with the Old Quad* (top right), *the National Library, Sheriff Court, and Bank of Scotland* (bottom left).

20. *In Parliament Square: Charles II, and the crown of St Giles.*

II. THE ROYAL MILE

Parliament Square always has a secluded air, being protected from the workaday bustle of the Royal Mile by the bulk of St Giles. The proximity of the august law courts, too, may engender a certain awed respect in the passer-by. The equestrian statue of Charles II heightens the dramatic contrast between the neo-classical ornaments of the Parliament House, and the Gothic traceries of St Giles.

The statue was cast in Holland and, though artistically satisfying, retains an aura of mystery. Why, for example, was Charles given the role of a Roman general wearing a chaplet of laurel? Why is his expression so contrary to what one would expect of a king dubbed the 'Merry Monarch'? Why has he no stirrups? And so on. One story has it that the statue was originally meant to be Cromwell and that the head was hastily switched at the Restoration. Another says that it represents the Duke of Parma. All that is known for certain is that it was completed in 1685, just before the death of Charles, and is probably the oldest lead equestrian statue in Britain.

With the exception of the Castle, no building in the Capital has been the centre of more turbulence and drama through the centuries than the High Kirk, St Giles. This is difficult to appreciate as one approaches the building, because of the unfortunate style in which the exterior was restored in 1829. Above the drab walls, however, can be seen the handsome fifteenth-century crown tower, and its rugged stones give a more accurate hint of what is to be found within. The old battle flags over the aisles, the soaring stained glass, the memorials in the shadows —all testify to the role of St Giles as National Church as well as parish kirk.

There has been a church on this site since the ninth century, but only the four central pillars survived an English raid in 1385. Three chapels in the present building date from 1387. In a charter which has never been revoked, Charles II made St Giles a cathedral, but it is not the seat of a bishop. In its time the building has been made to play many roles, not all of them dignified. In 1571 the Scottish commander, Kirkcaldy of Grange, stationed a detachment of troops in the tower. In the late sixteenth and early seventeenth centuries, because of Edinburgh's rapid increase in population, the church was partitioned and pressed into service as grammar school, courts of justice, police office, town clerk's office, prison, and weaver's workshop. It is said that the city gallows were stowed in one corner. Later, as the need for churches increased, the building was subdivided into four separate kirks, each with its own congregation.

St Giles is imperishably associated with the ministry of John Knox, the Protestant Reformer, who lies buried somewhere in Parliament Square. Knox stood at the very centre of the theological storm which went on until, in 1560, the Kirk of Scotland was reformed. It was during this tempestuous period that St Giles lost a famous relic. Said to have been the arm-bone of the saint, it had been given to the church in 1454 by Preston of Gorton. It rested in a gold mount and had a diamond ring on its finger, and on 1 September each year it was ceremoniously borne through the city. In 1557 a mob seized it and cast it into the Nor' Loch. By the seventeenth century, the campaign against Rome was won, but Presbyterian freedom was now threatened by episcopacy. Charles I decreed that churches should read the English liturgy, and St Giles's most famous dissident was Jenny Geddes, who is said to have hurled her stool at the Dean during a service.

As Scotland's National Church, St Giles plays its part in the ceremonies which mark the opening of the annual General Assembly of the Church of Scotland. By tradition, the Queen appoints as her representative at the General Assembly the Lord High Commissioner, who walks in procession from St Giles to open the Assembly.

The Assembly, which is attended by representative ministers and elders, is the supreme court of the Kirk of Scotland; and it discusses in the Assembly Hall a wide range of topics of international as well as national importance. The first Assembly was in 1560, when the redoubtable John Knox is said to have been one of six ministers present. Today the Fathers and Brethren at the Assembly number some 1,400.

A twentieth-century addition to St Giles is the elaborate Thistle Chapel, designed by Sir Robert Lorimer. The Order of the Thistle is Scotland's premier Order of Chivalry and one of the interesting features of the Chapel are the personal crests, over the stalls, of the Knights of the Order. The crests include that of the Queen, who is the only woman to have been nominated to the Order.

'If we exclude Russia', wrote the late Lord Cooper, 'two great schools of legal thought have latterly been contending for the allegiance of the modern world', namely the Anglo-American, 'founded upon English common law and equity', and the Continental, 'founded on the law of Rome': but Scots law still 'occupies a position somewhere midway between the two great opposing schools'.

In his *Memorials* (1856), Lord Cockburn recalls one ancient abuse which still prevailed even in 1800. 'At Edinburgh, the old judges had a practice at which even their barbaric age used to shake its head. They had always wine and biscuits *on the bench*, when the business was clearly to be protracted beyond the usual dinner hour. . . . Black bottles of strong port were set down beside them on the bench, with glasses, caraffes of water, tumblers, and biscuits; and this without the slightest attempt at concealment. The refreshment was generally allowed to stand untouched, and as if despised, for a short time, during which their Lordships seemed to be intent only on their notes. But in a little, some water was poured into the tumbler, and sipped quietly as if merely to sustain nature. Then a few drops of wine were ventured upon, but only with the water: till at last patience could endure no longer, and a full bumper of the pure black element was tossed over; after which the thing went on regularly, and there was a comfortable munching and quaffing, to the great envy of the parched throats in the gallery.' But times have changed; and all such practices were for ever abolished in Lord Cockburn's own lifetime.

22. *Preceded by two macers, the Lord President and the Lord Justice Clerk lead their fellow Senators of the College of Justice back to the Parliament House after being kirked in St Giles.*

23. *The Lord High Commissioner addressing the General Assembly of the Kirk of Scotland.*

24. *The Lord Lyon King of Arms entering St Giles at the opening of the General Assembly.*

The City Mace, traditionally borne in procession before the Lord Provost as a symbol of power, was made in 1617 by an Edinburgh goldsmith, George Robertson. It is over three feet long and of silver gilt, the upper portion of the bell head being styled as a crown. The use of the mace originated with the Romans, who paraded bundles of rods, with axes in the centre, before their consuls and praetors. In 1609, James VI granted a charter ordering Edinburgh Magistrates to carry and bear bundles of rods and such ensigns before them as signs and tokens of their magistracy. The charter also granted the Lord Provost the right to have a sword carried before him. It was not, however, until 1627 that Charles I presented the sword still in use.

The Lord Provost's badge and chain of office, with the city motto NISI DOMINUS FRUSTRA (*i.e.*, 'Unless the Lord [watches over the city, the watchman stays awake] in vain'), was first worn in 1899 by Lord Provost Sir Mitchell Thomson. The gold chain has a centre link with the letters E facing each other, joined by a heart of laurel, representing the Heart of Midlothian. The jewel has 470 brilliants and 22 rose diamonds.

25, 26. *The City Regalia, including the Lord Provost's elaborate Chain of Office, and the magnificent Mace, presented by James VI, and Sword of State.*

The exact origins of the Edinburgh Town Council are open to speculation. According to existing records, the first known official of Edinburgh was William de Dederyck, alderman, who signed the Ragman Roll in 1296. A bailie is mentioned in 1344, the Dean of Guild in 1410; and the Provost, Bailies, and Council were first mentioned in 1447. Some of the Burgh Laws, which are attributed to David 1 (1124-53), provided, however, that each burgh was to have a body of twelve men 'to preserve and maintain the laws and customs of the burgh'. If the Town Council of Edinburgh grew up out of one of these bodies, it must be more than 800 years old.

During the reign of King James II (1437-60), Edinburgh came to hold the position of chief burgh. Sir Alexander Napier of Merchiston was Provost then, and he subsequently served in other important posts, notably as Ambassador to England, and as Vice-Admiral.

In 1603, Admiralty jurisdiction over the Port of Leith was bestowed on the Provost, Magistrates, and Town Council. Although the Provost was never officially granted the title of 'Admiral of the Firth of Forth', this rank came to be given to successive holders of the office. In fact, until 1914, the Lord Provost of Edinburgh sometimes issued passports for foreign travel as 'Lord Provost of the City of Edinburgh, High Sheriff within the same and the Liberties thereof, one of H.M. Justices of the Peace for the County of Midlothian, Admiral of the Firth of Forth'.

As Edinburgh grew in importance, so did the functions of the Town Council. The magistrates wielded great power within the city boundary, extending, in the early days, even to the right of life and death over citizens. Early in the eighteenth century, Edinburgh ceased to be confined within the Flodden Wall, and began to expand southwards. Then, under the inspiration of Lord Provost George Drummond, a Highlander, who held office six times during the mid-eighteenth century, the City crossed the Nor' Loch, and began building its New Town. Drummond was both a visionary and a practical man, and of all the Lord Provosts the City has had, he is probably the best known. It was he who laid the foundation-stone of the old North Bridge (1763); and the elegance of the New Town is a daily reminder of him.

The Town Council has 71 members, including Town Councillors, who are elected by the citizens on the basis of three for each of the city's 23 wards. The other two members of the Council are the Lord Dean of Guild (appointed by the Guildry of the City), and the Convener of Trades (appointed by the Incorporated Trades), who can vote only at committee meetings, not at full Council meetings.

From among the 69 Councillors are appointed the Lord Provost, the Treasurer, (who is Chairman of the Finance Committee and guides the City's financial policy), 10 Bailies (i.e., magistrates), and up to 11 Judges of Police, who assist the Bailies by taking turns with them on the Bench in the Burgh Court.

The local government of Scotland's capital extends from such essential services as lighting, sanitation, and traffic, to the recent establishment of a Civic Theatre, and the continuance and encouragement of the world-famous Edinburgh Festival. The Edinburgh that has emerged from two world wars is more conscious than ever of its position, not only in relation to Scotland, but to the world as a whole. Unlike the introspective Edinburgh of Victorian times, it looks outwards and welcomes visitors from over the globe.

27. *In the City Chambers, the Lord Provost presides over a meeting of the Town Council.*

28. *In the Parliament Hall: the impressive oak roof was constructed in the mid-seventeenth century.*

29. *In the Parliament Hall: Roubiliac's magnificent statue of Duncan
Forbes of Culloden (1685-1748), Lord President of the Court of
Session, laying down the law.* Crown copyright: all rights reserved.

31. *In the High Street, early in the day: the sixteenth-century gabled building in the centre of the picture is said to have been John Knox's house.*

30. *In the High Street, during the afternoon: the Tron Kirk and St Giles, from the Fountain Well.*

32. Balcony and gateway of Moray House, in the Canongate.

According to legend, the heavily-trussed balcony of Moray House has supported spectators at two of Edinburgh's most historic events.

The house (now part of Edinburgh's College of Education), was built about 1628 by the widow of the first Earl of Home, who then presented it to her daughter Margaret, wife of the fourth Earl of Moray. Lady Home was a staunch supporter of the enemies of Charles I and contributed handsomely to the cause of the Covenanters.

The most famous event concerning the balcony occurred on 18 May 1650. On that day Lord Lorne, later the Earl of Argyll, his bride, and their wedding party crowded on to the balcony to watch the Marquis of Montrose being led past on his way to imprisonment and execution. Montrose, Argyll's arch enemy, had been taken by the Covenanters after the battle of Invercarron and brought across the Forth at Leith. Montrose's stately bearing during this ordeal silenced the heckling crowds; and it is said that when Argyll's lady spat at Montrose, Argyll himself turned away. Later Argyll, his son, and several other members of the wedding party traversed the same route on their way to an identical fate.

At the time of the Treaty of Union, Moray House was the residence of the Earl of Seafield, the Lord High Chancellor, and one of the commissioners for the negotiation of the Treaty. In the arbour behind the house, part of the Treaty was signed, and from the balcony, spectators saw the last riding [procession] of the Scottish Parliament.

44

33. *Seventeenth-century carving: Bible Land, also in the Canongate.*

1677

Ehold how good a thing it is
and how becoming well
Together such as brethren are
in unity to dwell

'TIS AN HONOUR FOR MEN TO CEASE FROM STRIF

34. *Advocates' Close.*   35. *Bakehouse Close.*

36. *Fisher's Close.*   37. *Tweeddale Court.*

38. *Mother's-eye view, in James Court.*

39. *The back street.* →

40. *'. . . or I'll skelp yer lug t'ye!'* →

One's first reaction might be that a close called 'World's End' had been named by a prophet of doom. The explanation, in fact, is more simple and without apocalyptic implications.

Looking now at the mile-long expanse between the Castle and Holyrood Palace, it is necessary to remember that officially Edinburgh once ended at what is now St Mary's Street. This was the site of the Nether Bow Port; and the close was the last alley within the city wall. It was for that reason that someone jauntily christened it the 'Warld's End'. Beyond was the autonomous burgh of Canongate. Other cities used the same appellation; Londoners gave the title to a public house at what they thought the edge of their civilisation.

Brass markers across the High Street at this point commemorate the exact position and shape of the Nether Bow. It was a very narrow gateway, scarcely wider than the average motor car. Because of modern traffic, it can be hazardous to make more than a kerbside examination. On the wall of the tenement on the north side of the street, however, can be seen an excellent bronze relief of the Nether Bow Port as it once was. Here, too, ran the Flodden Wall, hastily erected by the city after the disastrous Scottish defeat of 1513.

World's End Close twice assumed other names. For a time it was called Swift's Close after a man who owned the foreland house in it in 1595, and in the seventeenth century it became known as Stanfield's Close. The latter designation gave the passage a brief spell of notoriety because of the murder of Sir John Stanfield, who occupied a house at the foot of the close.

Sir John was found drowned in 1687 in suspicious circumstances. Suspicion increased after a hasty burial, for which, some said, his wife produced ready-made grave clothes. The body was exhumed; and, after making one incision in the neck, the examining physicians concluded that Sir John had died by strangulation and again prepared the corpse for burial. Sir John's son, who had been present during the examination, helped them to lift the corpse into the coffin and, during the transfer, blood gushed out on to his hands. Stricken with terror, the son withdrew and refused to touch the body. By this act, he was held to have revealed his guilt. In the legal phraseology accepted at that time, this was known as the 'ordeal by touch'. The son was subsequently executed; but the case provoked so much controversy that 'ordeal by touch' was never again accepted as proof of guilt in Scotland.

41. *In Dunbar's Close, off the Canongate, this glimpse of the neo-classical architecture of the Royal High School provides a characteristic contrast.*

Early morning is an excellent time of day at which to explore Edinburgh. Then the traffic is reduced and one is allowed to obtain a true impression of the shape of streets and buildings. In the light of the rising sun, familiar landscapes take on a new aspect. The sunlit steeple of the Tron Church, for example, stands out in sharp contrast to the image it casts on Hogmanay, or Old Year's Night. Then, to waiting revellers, the grey stone is only a background to the hands of the clock as they approach midnight.

The Tron Church traditionally is one of the social hubs of Edinburgh. Erected in 1637, the Church takes its name from the Tron [public weighing beam], which stood near its door. Vendors used the site to sell their wares, and its popularity as a meeting place led naturally to the custom of seeing in the New Year beneath its spire. The original Dutch bell-tower was destroyed in the great fire which ravaged this part of Edinburgh in 1824, and the existing spire was built in the nineteenth century.

Opposite the Tron Church stands the National Commercial Bank. In a cellar below the bank, it is alleged, some of the articles of the Anglo-Scottish Union of 1707 were signed—the Commissioners having been forced to take refuge there after being pursued from Moray House by a mob of infuriated citizens.

Down the slope from the Bank is an area formerly known as the Fountain district of the High Street, owing to the presence of a handsomely-walled fountain or well. Several street-wells still standing in the thoroughfare to-day are the relics of the notable project of 1681, when a pipe laid from Comiston gave the High Street a proper water supply. From the street-wells, porters who were known as caddies carried water up to the high houses for housewives, the charge being a halfpenny per bucket.

At the foot of Fountain Close stands St Patrick's Catholic Church, which originally was the Library of the College of Physicians. In this close, too, Thomas Bassendyne printed the first translation of the New Testament to be published in Scotland; he had already printed an edition of the works of Sir David Lyndsay, whose *Satire of the Thrie Estatis* was produced, to universal acclaim, at the second Edinburgh Festival. Bassendyne died in Fountain Close in 1577.

The many closes up and down the High Street were originally small strips of gardens adjacent to private homes. With a continued increase in population on the ridge running from the Castle, buildings expanded upwards and the closes became passage ways instead of gardens. There were gardens, however, on the slopes of the ridge. Tweeddale Close, for example, had a large plantation of lime trees and, later, gardens which extended down to the Cowgate.

Tweeddale Court today is bisected by large cast-iron gates which frame the entrance to the offices of Oliver and Boyd, the publishers of this book. Just inside the gates one can still see a lean-to shelter once used to store sedan chairs.

At one time the head office of the British Linen Bank was located in this close; and here, in November 1806, William Begbie, a bank-messenger, was robbed and murdered while returning from the Leith branch. It is recorded that the assault was accomplished with the 'utmost deliberation', but the murderer was never found.

Located in the Fountain district too is one of the Corporation's newer museums—the Museum of Childhood. Beneath the sign of the gargoyle and toy soldier the visitor may retrace his steps to childhood by means of the historical collection of toys, costumes and books.

52

44. *Victoria Street, south of the Lawnmarket, leads down from George IV Bridge to the foot of the old West Bow.*

Edinburgh's sudden declines and abrupt ascents called for inventive building methods. Thus one encounters an abundance of cut-through closes, stairway wynds, and houses built on levels, with the main door at the top and an inside staircase descending to the livingroom. The building of terraced streets, such as Victoria Street and Terrace, south of the Lawnmarket, is an example of inspired adaptation to the existing topography.

Another distinctive feature of residential buildings in the Old Town is their height. It has been said that seventeenth-century Edinburgh, rather than New York, invented the skyscraper. Certainly, Edinburgh led the Continent in the construction of multi-storey buildings, one example being a fourteen-storey wall of houses, which until the beginning of the last century lined the back of what is now called Parliament Square. Most of these structures were reduced by fire and alteration. It is still possible, however, to appreciate the towering effect of such buildings of the eighteenth century by walking through Lady Stair's Close, leading from the Mound to the Lawnmarket, and craning one's head upwards.

45. *Tenements and shop fronts, in the Lawnmarket.*

The reason for building skywards was one of defence. Men were afraid to leave the easily-defended slope of the Castle Rock and they clustered along the ridge, building upwards instead of outwards. The worst side-effect of this crowded living was the lack of sanitation.

Johnson's remark to Boswell on the former's first evening in Edinburgh sums up the state of the city's streets in the eighteenth century. 'I smell you in the dark', the famous traveller said to his companion; and the remark was, if anything, an understatement. At this time, Edinburgh still resembled a medieval city and the population of 60,000 was too great for such a small area. The phrase 'Gardyloo', from the French '*Garde à l'eau*', was a familiar evening chant as buckets of refuse were thrown out the window to the discomfiture of any slow-footed strollers below. The building of one house upon another added to the scene of squalor and even people of wealth were forced to live in confined spaces. These were often airless, windowless rooms, or hovels below street level, and in such conditions epidemics of typhus fever and cholera were inevitable.

The worst visitation of the plague took place in 1645, when it is said that the High Street was almost deserted. In Leith that same year, less than one in three survived the epidemic. In 1721, when the Town Council applied to the College of Physicians for advice on sanitary measures against a possible outbreak of the plague, the doctors advised that refuse carts should be provided to clean the streets, the Nor' Loch drained, and beggars removed. Again in 1831, when cholera was sweeping westward from Asia, the Commissioners of Police hastily prepared the city by cleaning the closes and streets, removing pigs, and providing food and clothes for the poor. Still, when the cholera arrived 600 people died in six months. There were other epidemics in 1848 and 1849, and the fear continued for some years after.

A major-turning point in the city's development of proper sanitation methods followed the collapse of a tenement in Chalmer's Close in 1861, when 35 people died. Today, the archway leading into the Close bears a sculptured head in memory of the lad who shouted resolutely to his rescuers from beneath the rubble, 'Heave awa, lads, I'm no deid yet'. After this incident the Town Council appointed its first Officer of Health, Dr Henry Littlejohn, who prepared an exhaustive report on the city's sanitary conditions. In 1867 came the historic Improvement Act, which was aimed at deploying the population then concentrated along the Royal Mile.

55

46. *Chessel's Court, where Deacon Brodie committed the last of his many crimes, has now been restored by the Corporation.*

Chessel's Court, which is seen to advantage from the arcade supporting the Royal Mile frontage, is one of several restorations which the Corporation recently carried out in the Canongate. This eighteenth-century building, once the Excise Office, now provides a total of eighteen modern flats converted by Robert Hurd & Partners.

The Excise Office witnessed the downfall of a notorious character, Deacon Brodie. William Brodie was a Deacon of Wrights and Masons of Edinburgh and a Deacon Councillor of the city, who practised his trade of cabinet-making in the Lawnmarket. His appearance was most respectable yet he secretly cultivated a *penchant* for gambling which put him in bad company. After a series of robberies, which culminated in a raid on the Excise Office, Deacon Brodie was apprehended, tried, sentenced to death, and hanged. Ironically, the sentence was pronounced in a courtroom in which he had recently acted as a juryman.

56

Another residential showplace in the restored Canongate is Whitehorse Close. Tradition says that the Close, because of its proximity to Holyrood Palace, was used to stable Queen Mary's horses, and that it was named after a white palfry owned by the Queen. Later, the Close served as a rendezvous for passengers travelling to London; the White Horse Inn, the building with the Y-shaped staircase at the rear of the Close, was the point of departure for stage coaches.

The Royal Commission on Ancient Monuments has described the Close as a 'unique survival from the seventeenth century'—unique, one imagines, because it escaped the sky-scraping expansion which changed the appearance of so many other buildings in the Royal Mile. Despite major alterations to the interiors, the outer appearance of the Close remains the same, and on one dormer window in the courtyard is the date 1623.

The White Horse Inn so captured the imagination of Sir Walter Scott that he used it in the Waverley novels. In the restoration of the Close, which took over three years and cost £65,000, the old stables were converted into garages and the Canongate frontage adapted to form a shopping arcade. Nineteen houses resulted from the restoration.

47. *White Horse Close, once a well-known coaching inn, has also been modernised.*

Not long after the end of the Second World War, the City decided to embark upon a massive and courageous rescue operation in the Royal Mile. The old street, which had witnessed so much of Scotland's history, had fallen on evil days. True, a notable building here and there had been saved from ruin, but the general scene, particularly in the Canongate, was one of crumbling slum property, shuttered shops, brick-strewn sites, and a departed glory.

The tide of opinion was slow in turning, for at first few seemed convinced of the feasibility of reviving the corpse. Perhaps the most celebrated of the early rescuers was the fourth Marquess of Bute, who in the mid-1930s bought Acheson House (1633), the last of Edinburgh's courtyard mansions, and commissioned a young architect to restore it. The architect was Robert Hurd, who was destined to play such a prominent part in later, more ambitious restoration projects.

Public interest was slowly stimulated in the cause, which had two objects: to preserve examples of historic Scottish vernacular architecture; and, even more important, to restore a vigorous community life to the Royal Mile.

The Corporation sponsored a survey of the whole street by the City Architect of the time, E. J. MacRae, and his recommendations were subsequently incorporated in the exciting city-wide survey of 1949, carried out for the Corporation by Sir Patrick Abercrombie. The lean years were at last drawing to their close.

The Canongate, which extends from St Mary's Street to Holyrood, takes its name from the Augustine monks of Holyrood. The monks, or canons, were permitted to settle a village under a charter granted by David I in 1128. The main street of the village took their name with the addition of the Scots word 'gate', meaning 'way'. The Canongate remained a separate burgh, with its own magistrates, until 1856, when it was incorporated into Edinburgh.

The Canongate was always less congested than the neighbouring High Street of Edinburgh, the main reason being that it lay outside the city wall. Lord Cockburn, in *Memorials of His Time* (1856) gives a glimpse of the Canongate in an era long gone. Recalling impressions from his childhood, Cockburn wrote of the pleasant gardens, the woods, and the noble residents.

Cockburn wrote wistfully of the Canongate, but its real days of glory far preceded his own time. The decline had actually begun in 1603 when James VI succeeded to the throne of England and the Court was removed from Edinburgh. There followed the Parliamentary Union of 1707, and the building of the New Town, both of which added to its neglect. Still, in the middle of the eighteenth century many people of note continued to linger in the Canongate. In *Old and New Edinburgh* (1882), James Grant recorded a 'curious list' of Canongate residents, which he had obtained from Mr Robert Chalmers, who had obtained it from Mr Chalmers Izett, 'whose memory extended back to 1769'. According to Mr Izett, Canongate residents then included two dukes, sixteen earls, two dowager countesses, seven lords, seven lords of session, thirteen baronets, four commanders of the forces in Scotland, and five eminent men.

With restoration of the physical environment, the Royal Mile community is once again being established—and apparently on the egalitarian lines of old. Many in professional and public life are among the residents of the modernised flats. The old street has a new vitality and the achievement has been recognised with awards from the Saltire Society, the Civic Trust, and other amenity societies. The financial cost has been heavy, but no true Scot now would grudge it.

58

48. *Old tenements, beside the Canongate Tolbooth, before the Corporation renovated them.*

49. *The Old Town, with modern municipal development at Dumbiedykes, from the Radical Road.*

50. *Children's playground: Dumbiedykes.*

Happy hearts and happy faces,
Happy play in grassy places—
That was how, in ancient ages,
Children grew to kings and sages.

To most adults, Robert Louis Stevenson is synonymous with childhood—with the imaginary figures of Long John Silver, David Balfour, and Alan Breck; and the simple, yet expressive, nursery rhymes like the verse above from 'Good and Bad Children', in *A Child's Garden of Verses*.

Stevenson was born on 13 November 1850 at 8 Howard Place, opposite the Botanic Gardens; and, though he lived into his forty-fifth year, he retained his boyhood heart. He was a sickly, only child who was coddled, and even quoted, by an adoring mother. His father, a lighthouse engineer, was the frequent host of retired sea captains and lighthouse-keepers and these guests undoubtedly captured young Robert's imagination. He was an indifferent student, given to occasional practical jokes. But his exceptional charm, which his many biographers emphasise, seems to have carried him over any difficult escapades. Another important characteristic of his personality was high spirit—somehow, despite a lifetime of illness, he retained his good humour and blithesomeness.

Treasure Island was Stevenson's first and most instant success. He wrote it while staying at Braemar, for the amusement of his stepson, interspersing the composition of the adventure story with the writing of verses. But Stevenson, while primarily judged as a children's author, had a great *penchant* for the mysterious, which he effectively demonstrated in *Dr Jekyll and Mr Hyde*. *Weir of Hermiston* was his last and most serious work. It was based on Lord Braxfield, the hanging judge, and was aptly prejudged, by the author, as his masterpiece. This prediction was true, despite the fact that the work was unfinished when Stevenson died in 1894.

51. *Children's playground: Victoria Terrace.*

Little remains of the almost Z-shaped West Bow, which dropped from the Lawnmarket down to the Grassmarket, connecting the High Town and the Low Town. During the building of Victoria Street between 1835 and 1840, it was all but obliterated, taking with it a colourful era in Edinburgh history.

The atmosphere of the West Bow was essentially festive. The street was lined with tall, antique houses with dovecot-like gables, full of small sculptures, and was the passage by which royalty entered the city. Ceremonial pageants were often held on these occasions. The streets also contained the shops of many iron-smiths and tin-smiths. Some of these craftsmen—men of great piety—were dubbed the Bow-head Saints. The sanctity of the neighbourhood, it appeared at the time, was enhanced when Major Weir—or 'Angelical Thomas'—took up residence.

To all appearances Major Weir was a man of exemplary character. His black-cloaked figure, staff in hand, was seen frequently up and down the West Bow. The Major led a devoted life, as did his sister Grizel, with whom he shared his home. At the age of 70, however, Weir began confessing to a series of monstrous crimes and, though the Lord Provost at first refused to believe him, he was taken into custody and tried. Both Weir and his sister were condemned to death —she to be hanged in the Grassmarket, he to be strangled and burnt between Leith and Edinburgh.

Burnt with the Major was his mysterious staff, which had achieved notoriety through its strange properties. People said it often preceded the Major as he walked down the street, and was quite capable of delivering a letter or answering the door. For a century after his execution in 1670, the Major's house in West Bow remained empty—and a source of great fear. Strange lights were seen within.

In 1710 the first Assembly Room opened in the West Bow, much to the annoyance of pious neighbours, for many Presbyterians then considered 'promiscuous dancing' frivolous, if not sinful, although most Jacobites, on the whole, approved of it. On one occasion a rabble assaulted the Assembly Room and perforated the door with red-hot spits. As Oliver Goldsmith later reported, such conservatives might have been surprised had they gone indoors while a dance was in progress. According to Goldsmith, all the ladies remained on one side of the room and all the gentlemen on the other. A lady director matched the partners to 'walk a minuet' or for country dancing, and no one spoke. Some years later, when the Assembly Room had reopened after a brief recess, a sign by the door cautioned: 'No lady to be admitted in a night-gown, and no gentleman in boots'.

The West Bow, which was the route taken by the condemned on their way to execution in the Grassmarket, was the scene of the Porteous riots in 1736. During the execution of a smuggler in the Grassmarket schoolboys started throwing stones at the hangman. John Porteous, captain of the city guard, ordered his men to fire on the crowd and six people were killed. Porteous was subsequently convicted by a jury and condemned; just before his execution, however, he was reprieved by Queen Caroline, then Regent. This action so infuriated the people of Edinburgh that on the night before Porteous was to have been hanged, they disarmed the City Guard and blocked up the gates to the city. Porteous was taken from his cell and hustled down the West Bow, the mob stopping only to buy some rope. As soon as Porteous was hanged, the crowd dispersed quietly. The Queen was outraged, and the Lord Provost of Edinburgh was taken into custody. The organisers of this well-planned scheme were never traced.

52. *The Royal Infirmary* (top left), *the McEwan Hall* (top right),
George Square, and the Hume Tower.

53. *Tolbooth St John's and St Giles, from the Old Quad.*

III. THE REST OF THE OLD TOWN

The Old College of Edinburgh University, in the South Bridge, was designed in 1789 by Robert Adam. The original plan was masterly and promised to fulfil the great architect's ambition to erect a notable public building. It featured an elaborate portico leading to a transverse forecourt and hence into a large quadrangle. Unfortunately, before the portico and northwest corner of the quadrangle had even neared completion, Adam died, and within a year all work had ceased. For more than twenty years, work on the College was almost negligible, mainly because of lack of funds. Finally in 1815 Parliament granted £10,000 a year to complete the buildings, and W. H. Playfair, the architect, succeeded to Adam's job.

As a result of Playfair's modifications, the Old College today is one large court of both Palladian and Grecian design. The dome, designed about 1880 by Sir R. Rowand Anderson, is larger than the one originally envisaged.

The outstanding interior within the Old College is the Upper Library, also designed by Playfair. The central gallery is lined with pillared bays, for books, on each side. The most important collection in the library is one gifted by David Laing in 1878.

54. *The Castle, from the Vennel.*

Cauld blaws the nippin north wi' angry sough,
And showers his hailstanes frae the Castle *Cleugh   *cliff
O'er the Grayfriars, whare, at mirkest hour,
Bogles and spectres wont to tak their tour . . . .

So wrote Edinburgh's own poet, Robert Fergusson, in 'The Ghaists: A Kirk-yard Eclogue'. His word-picture of the cold north wind is readily appreciated by Edinburgh folk, who learned long ago to adopt a huddled stance against its penetration. Snow comes infrequently to the lower reaches of the city. But the Castle Rock, Arthur's Seat, and the Pentland Hills are more easily covered—much to the delight of Edinburgh's children, who used to welcome the wintry air with the jingle

Aa the hills are covered wi snaw
An Winter's nou come fairly.

In singling out the north wind, Fergusson captured the essence of winter in the capital city. But then, he knew his Edinburgh well. Fergusson was born in Edinburgh in 1750 near the Tron Kirk, and when he died only twenty-four years later he left behind some thirty Scots poems—enough to prove his youthful genius.

In his early years Fergusson attended first an elementary school and later the High School of Edinburgh. His father William must undoubtedly have exerted a strong educational influence on him; for he was a clerk in the British Linen Company; one of his grandfathers had been a minister, and he himself had written poetry in his youth. At the age of twelve, Robert was given a bursary and went to Dundee Grammar School. He later moved on to St Andrews University, but left it without having graduated.

In appearance, Fergusson has been described as about 5 ft. 9 in. in height, with a pale complexion, light brown hair, and a vivacious temperament. From the first, his poor health was apparent, but his nature was attractive, and in his student days he was given to playing practical jokes.

After leaving St Andrews, he took a job as a copyist in Edinburgh and soon gathered a circle of friends about him. At this particular juncture in history, tavern clubs provided the chief source of entertainment for an evening's outing, and Fergusson was nominated to the famous Cape Club, which met in the Isle of Man Tavern in Craig's Close, just above Cockburn Street. Another member was the painter Raeburn. Fergusson had achieved public popularity with his poems written in Scots, having earlier made a first attempt at writing in English, and this, plus his own amiable character, made him much in demand as an entertainer.

Sadly, the people who sought his company most, conveniently neglected him in his last days. At the age of twenty-three, Fergusson became subject to long bouts of depression, which finally culminated in his being sent to a madhouse, where he died in 1774. His achievement in his few years was remarkable, and we are left wondering what poetry would have come from his pen, had he been granted even a few more years. His eulogy was left to his pupil Burns, who some years later applied for permission to place a stone on Fergusson's unmarked grave. As related by James Grant in *Old and New Edinburgh* (1882), Burns was told that he could not mark the grave without the permission of the financial managers of the Canongate Kirk fund; and he replied, 'Tell them it is the Ayrshire ploughman who makes the request'. The stone is there still, in the Canongate Kirk graveyard.

67

55. *The dome of the Old Quad.*

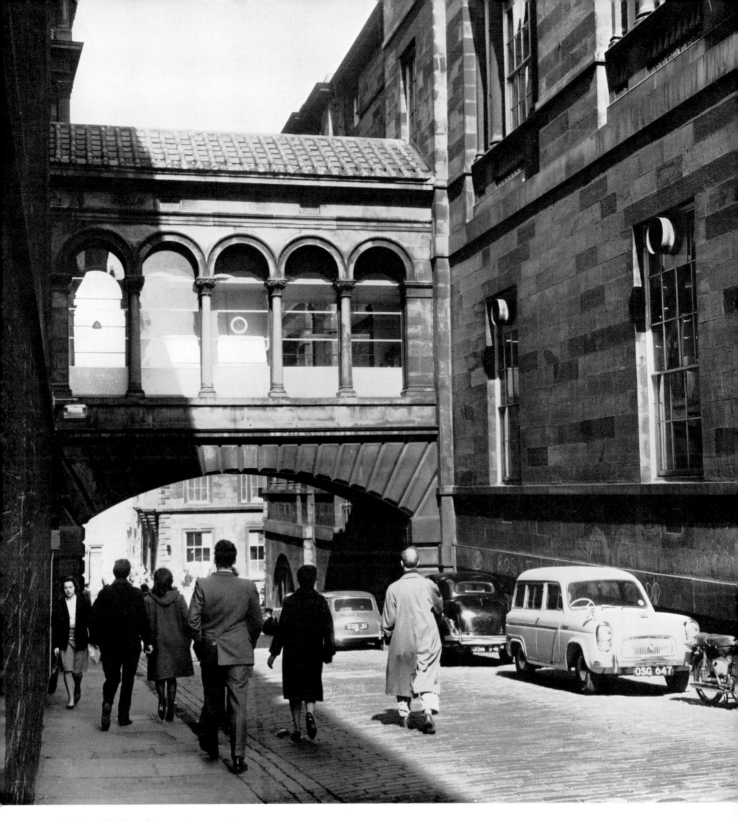

56. *West College Street, in term-time.*

A decision made by the Town Council on 14 April 1582 gave the city its proudest institution, one which was destined to bestow profound humanitarian benefits upon the farthest corners of the world.

Edinburgh University was born when the Town Council gave instructions for 'the funding and bigging [building] of ane college for lettres in the Kirk of Feild'. It was an uneasy period, for religious controversy raged throughout the country, but the founding of the 'Tounis College' was in keeping with the democratic concept of universal free education envisaged by the Protestant reformers.

Scotland has three older universities—St Andrews, Glasgow, and Aberdeen —but Edinburgh eventually became the largest and best-known of the four. In 1966 the city acquired a second university, when the Heriot-Watt College was given university status. It was founded as mechanics institute early in the nineteenth century and over the years earned for itself a distinguished reputation in technological fields.

Edinburgh University opened in hastily-constructed buildings at the Kirk o' Field—scene of the unsolved murder of Henry Darnley, husband of Mary Queen of Scots. There were eighty students under the tutelage of Robert Rollock, a former professor at St Andrews. To-day there are more than 7,000 students, and Rollock's original course in Philosophy has developed into six Faculties—Divinity, Law, Arts, Science, Music, and Medicine. The last-named has done more than any other to give the University its world wide reputation, and medical students come from every continent to acquire professional skills.

The University has made significant contributions in many fields of study: one recently has been in phonetics. The study of the spoken word is not new to Edinburgh. Alexander Melville Bell lectured at the University and wrote the book *Visible Speech*, which was published in 1867. His son, Alexander Graham Bell, the inventor of the telephone, was a student at the University. A stone in the wall on the west side of South Charlotte Street commemorates his birthplace.

Although the University's Department of Phonetics was not established until 1948, work in speech-analysis was already being done at the University as early as 1878. Then the experimenters were: Fleeming Jenkin, the Professor of Engineering; J. A. Ewing, who later became Principal; and Alexander Crum Brown, Professor of Chemistry. In 1942 an artificial talking-machine designed by Sir Richard Paget was demonstrated.

Today, a machine that is helping members of the Phonetics Department to obtain greater insight into the spoken word is the Parametric Artificial Talker— PAT for short. Originally developed and owned by the Ministry of Supply, PAT is capable of whispering, talking, and singing.

PAT talks by means of electrical circuits which resonate in a manner similar to the human vocal tract. Eight control signals or parameters, representing some of the elements present in human speech, are manipulated to help to produce the synthetic voice. Left to itself, the machine emits an undifferentiated sound. By manipulating one control, you can produce variations in pitch; by manipulating others, in loudness, vowel-quality, and hiss-frequency.

Although PAT is used solely for research at the University, its descendants could offer important benefits, not only in the field of speech but other areas as well. One day computers will probably speak their answers instead of writing them out, and machines will translate from one language to another.

57. *The Talking Machine.*

59. 'Inexplicable splendour of Ionian white and gold', in the Upper
Hall, Edinburgh University Library.

58. The Signet Library, designed by William Stark, belongs to the
Society of Writers to the Signet.

61. *Salisbury Crags and Arthur's Seat, from inside the Hume Tower.*

For years, Edinburgh's skyline was monopolised by the familiar silhouettes of the Castle, Arthur's Seat, and the Crown of St Giles. With the construction of the David Hume Tower, the city panorama acquired a striking contribution from the twentieth century.

The Hume Tower was the first stalwart shoot to grow from the University's development in George Square. It was fitting that it should be named in memory of the man whose mind has been described as perhaps the finest ever produced by Scotland. The association of Hume—historian, political economist, philosopher—with this structure of steel and glass is ironic; perhaps it is also a belated apology. For although *le bon David* attended Edinburgh University he never acquired a degree. Moreover, he was once refused the professorship of moral philosophy.

Hume was born in Edinburgh on 26 April 1711. He was destined for the law, but gave this up for a literary life which he pursued, for some years, in France. His *Treatise of Human Nature*, possibly 'the greatest work of philosophy in the English language', was published in 1739-40, but 'fell dead-born from the Press'. Although ignored by many of his own countrymen, Hume later enjoyed great success in Paris, where he was employed as secretary to the British Ambassador, and as *chargé d'affaires* (1764-66). After living for some time in London, which he disliked, he returned to Edinburgh in 1769; and in 1771 he settled down to live in St Andrew Square. In *My Own Life*, written a few months before his death in 1776, Hume described himself as having been 'a man of mild Dispositions, of Command of Temper, of an open, social, and cheerful Humour, . . . and of great Moderation in all my Passions'.

75

60. *The Hume Tower, George Square.*

Prior to the seventeenth century, Edinburgh people who needed medical treatment relied heavily on surgeon-apothecaries such as one Patrick Anderson, who developed a remedy for all diseases which he called 'Angelic Pills'. In the early 1600s, however, a group of Edinburgh physicians joined together informally for the purpose of producing medicinal herbs. This early liaison was the beginning of the Edinburgh University Medical School.

One of the pioneers in this experimentation with herbs was Sir Robert Sibbald. He and Dr Andrew Balfour started the first garden for growing herbs on a piece of ground belonging to Holyroodhouse, and there amassed about 900 plants—many of them from foreign countries. Later the garden was moved to land belonging to Trinity Hospital and its expansion was made possible with the help of donations. James Sutherland was put in charge of the Trinity Hospital Garden, and he eventually became the Professor of Botany at the College of Surgeons.

The College of Physicians was established on 29 November 1681, after several abortive attempts. The other Scottish universities of Scotland had concurred in its formulation but had laid down certain restrictive conditions, one being that the College should have no power to erect a medical school or confer degrees. In 1685, Sibbald, who was His Majesty's Physician, was appointed Professor of Physic in the College. Six months later, the Town Council chose Dr James Halket and Dr Archibald Pitcairne as Professors of Medicine. Some twenty-one years later, Sir Robert Sibbald announced that he would begin giving private courses of lectures.

63. *Rectorial Election, in the Old Quad.*

The practice of dissection had been legalised in Edinburgh in 1505; but no significant progress in this field was recorded for about two hundred years. In 1716, Adam Drummond and John McGill were appointed conjunctive professors of Anatomy in the College of Surgeons, succeeding Robert Elliot.

Development of the Medical School as an educational institution became a reality under Alexander Monro, *Primus*. Monro's father, John, a former Army surgeon, was president of the College of Surgeons in 1712-13. The senior Monro formed the idea of founding a seminary of medical education, and prepared his son to pursue this goal. As a youth, Alexander Monro was his father's apprentice. He watched the anatomy demonstrations of Drummond and McGill and at the age of twenty was sent to study anatomy in London, Paris, and Leyden, returning to Edinburgh two years later. His knowledge, even at this early stage, so impressed his professional seniors that McGill and Drummond resigned their conjunctive chair in his favour.

In 1721, Monro wrote a paper which advocated a public hospital for the study of practical medicine, and in 1738, owing to his influence and the efforts of Lord Provost George Drummond, the Royal Infirmary was begun—with six beds. It became one of the world's leading teaching hospitals.

Many well-known physicians have been associated with the Medical School. In 1869 Joseph Lister, one of the great pioneers in antiseptic surgery, became the third occupant of the Chair of Clinical Surgery. In 1840, Sir James Young Simpson the first to use chloroform, was appointed Professor of Midwifery. Another accomplished surgeon was Dr Joseph Bell, consultant to the Royal Infirmary and Royal Hospital for Sick Children. One medical student was so impressed by Dr Bell's powers of observation and diagnosis that he modelled one of the most famous characters in modern fiction on him: the student was Arthur Conan Doyle; the character, Sherlock Holmes.

77

62. *Medical students attending a lecture.*

Because of its hallowed associations, Greyfriars occupies a unique place among Scotland's burial grounds.

Greyfriars derives its name from a Franciscan monastery which once stood on the south side of the Grassmarket. In 1561, after the monastery had been dissolved, the Town Council petitioned the Crown to use the land as a burial ground, to relieve overcrowding in the churchyard of St Giles. When work began on the Greyfriars Kirk within the boundaries of the cemetery in 1612, it was the first church to be built in Edinburgh since the Reformation.

The most momentous event in the history of Greyfriars occurred there on 28 February 1638, when the National Covenant was signed. By this historic deed of signed assent, subscribed by nobles and common folk alike, the people of Scotland bound themselves to defend the person of King Charles I, but to reject completely his policy of enforcing episcopacy upon Scotland. All day long people streamed into the churchyard to pledge support to the Presbyterian faith. Many wept as they signed and some used their own blood as ink. A flat tombstone in the kirkyard is associated with the signing of the document.

At the height of the religious persecutions by the Stuart Kings, the churchyard became an open-air prison. Over 1,200 prisoners from the Battle of Bothwell Bridge (2 June 1679), were crowded into the south-west corner of the kirkyard from June to September. Many of the Covenanters died from starvation and exposure; others signed a bond not to take up arms against the Government; and still others met with death at sea, having been sold into slavery in the West Indies.

In 1718, the spire of Old Greyfriars Church was destroyed by an explosion of gunpowder, which had been put there by the town authorities for safe keeping. As the old building had already become too small for its congregation, it was decided to add a new kirk to the existing structure, instead of replacing the destroyed spire. New Greyfriars Church was started in 1721. The interiors of the two adjacent kirks were badly damaged by fire in 1845: but they were later restored; and the first organ ever to be used in a Scottish Presbyterian kirk was then installed. Finally, in 1937, the partition was removed and the congregation united.

The kirkyard is also notable for its unique collection of elaborate stone memorials. In the early days, authority to erect a monument had to be obtained from the Town Council; since the seventeenth century, the Dean of Guild has approved all building plans. Almost from the first the cemetery proved a popular repository with prominent Edinburgh citizens. It became overcrowded, a fact which prompted James Grant to record in his book, *Old and New Edinburgh*, in 1882: 'Here lie 37 chief magistrates of the city; 23 principals and professors of the University, . . . 33 of the most distinguished lawyers of their day, . . . six Lords President of the Supreme Court of Scotland; 22 senators of the College of Justice and a host of other distinguished men'.

The kirkyard, with its numerous memorial stones and curious iron structures for foiling body-snatchers, contains the mortal remains of many distinguished men. Buried here are William Carstares, adviser of William of Orange, and later Principal of Edinburgh University; the poet Allan Ramsay, author of *The Gentle Shepherd* and founder of Edinburgh's first lending library; the two Alexander Monros—*Primus* and *Secundus* (both holders of the Chair of Anatomy at the University); Sir Walter Scott's father; Duncan McIntyre, the Gaelic poet; and Duncan Forbes of Culloden, Lord President of the Court of Session. The Forbes memorial was not erected until 1949, having been commissioned two years earlier on the two-hundredth anniversary of his death. Other men buried in the kirkyard have achieved a different fame—Captain John Porteous, who provoked the Porteous Riot in 1736, and James Douglas, Earl of Morton, executed in 1581 for his role in the murder of Darnley.

One of the simplest monuments in the Greyfriars commemorates Walter Dunbar of Dykeside (1711-88), 'Who Supported his Rank in/life with probity, and Honour;/Felt, and practiced true Reli-/gion; and must long be remem/bered as an example of the wa-/rmth, and sincerity of Freendship'. One of the most magnificent encloses the remains of Sir George Mackenzie of Rosehaugh (1636-91), the Lord Advocate who prosecuted so many of the Covenanters. Boys used to insult his shade by going to the door of his tomb and shouting:

> Lift the sneck and draw the bar:
> Bluidie Mackingie, come out if ye daur!

64. *The Castle, the spire of Tolbooth St John's, and the Greyfriars Kirk and Kirkyard, from the south-east.*

65. *Tolbooth St John's, from the Greyfriars Kirkyard. The Martyrs' Monument* (third from the right) *commemorates the Covenanters executed in Edinburgh during the Killing Times.*

66. *Some of the ornate seventeenth-century tombs in the Greyfriars Kirkyard.*
One of the most conspicuous monuments in the Grey-friars Kirkyard is the obelisk, adorned with hunting trophies, which marks the grave of Duncan McIntyre (1724-1812), one of the best Scottish Gaelic poets. Here is a translation of the lines beginning FHIR THA D SHEASAMH AIR MO LIC, *which are inscribed on the base:*
Man, you who are standing on my tombstone,
I was the same as you are now:
Today my bed is the grave,
There's neither pith nor marrow in my bones.
Though you are young and strong,
You won't live for ever, despite
*   the reprieve you have got:*
Take my advice, be wise,
Remember often, death will come.

Donnchadh Bàn nan Oran [Fair-haired Duncan of the Songs] was born and bred in Glenorchy, but in 1766 he settled in Edinburgh, and joined the City Guard. In the words of one who knew him, 'he was, like all the rest of the poets, very fond of company and a cheerful glass, and was not only agreeable over his bottle but also very circumspect'.

67. *Greyfriars Bobby, with the Candlemakers' Hall in the background.*

Dogs are the subject of several memorials in the city. Maida, the faithful hound of Sir Walter Scott, lies at the author's feet in the Princes Street monument; and simple markers line the Castle plot where soldiers' pets were interred. The most famous, however, is Greyfriars Bobby.

In 1858, a shepherd from the Pentland Hills, named John Gray (Auld Jock) became ill and died suddenly during one of his weekly trips to Edinburgh. Friends made arrangements for his burial in Greyfriars Churchyard and returned his dog, a terrier, to the Pentlands farm where Gray had been employed. On the day following the burial, however, Bobby returned to his master's grave. The sight of his devotion touched the keeper of the kirkyard and Bobby soon became a favourite of local citizens. During the remaining fourteen years of his life, he stayed faithful to his master and haunted the kirkyard, spending much of his time resting on the grave itself. Once, when he was 'arrested' for not having a licence, the Lord Provost gave Bobby an engraved collar with a licence attached. Such was his fame that, on his death in 1872, Queen Victoria herself suggested he should be buried in the Greyfriars, near his master. The statue of Greyfriars Bobby, which stands at the top of Candlemaker Row, was erected by Baroness Burdett-Coutts.

One of the most striking monuments at Greyfriars is that erected in memory of James Borthwick, a surgeon-apothecary and prominent Edinburgh citizen who died in 1676. The monument displays a dancing skeleton holding a scythe and the Book of Destiny.

82

68. *Monument to James Borthwick of Stow, on the wall at the east end of Greyfriars Kirk.*

69. *A Johnnie A'thing, or general dealer's shop.*

The name of the Pleasance has an ironic ring. It is now an area of intensive development; and it is difficult to appreciate that it was once a place of trees and hedge-lined paths. Many people have assumed that it obtained its name from the gardens of the houses which once graced the nearby Cowgate. In fact, the explanation is more complicated; and the modern name seems to have been derived from 'St Mary of Piacenza's', or, in Latin, *Sanctae Mariae de Placentia*, the name of a Franciscan convent which was located in this part of Edinburgh before the Reformation. The district had previously been called 'Dearenough'.

The monastery of the Dominicans, or Black Friars, was also in this area, its boundaries being marked approximately by Drummond Street, the Pleasance, the Cowgate, and the South Bridge. The monastery was founded by Alexander II in 1230 and was the principal house of the Order in Scotland. It was built in quadrangle form with a large Gothic church, friars' cells, dormitories, dining hall, and library. In the centre of the square stood a fountain at which the friars are said to have performed their open-air ablutions. Unfortunately, nothing remains of the monastery.

The Cowgate, which runs east and west at the foot of the Pleasance, was originally a rustic lane between Holyrood and the Kirk of St Cuthbert. In the fifteenth century, however, it became a fashionable suburb populated by the nobility and officers of state who came to Edinburgh for assemblies and government meetings. The passage of time has destroyed these once fine buildings and little of interest remains. The street, however, still retains its own peculiar narrowness and sinuosity as it passes under the South Bridge and George IV Bridge into the Grassmarket. At the east end, and along Holyrood Road, are some of Edinburgh's breweries. Towards the west end stands the sixteenth century Magdalen Chapel with its notable pre-Reformation stained-glass window. Here was held the first General Assembly of the Church of Scotland.

70. *A double skipping game.*

The Pleasance took on an air of impoverishment in the eighteenth century. In the early days of its demise, Lady Jane Douglas, widow of Sir John Stewart of Grandtully, occupied a house near the junction of the Pleasance with St Leonard's. There she fought a long peerage case with the Duke of Hamilton, taking in washing to help to finance her domestic needs while looking after the son who was to become Lord Douglas of Douglas in 1790.

71. *Mary Queen of Scots Got her head chopped off!*

The Pleasance also proved a haven for the Society of Friends or Quakers. During the eighteenth century, their meetings in the town were frequently broken up by the Town Guard; on other occasions they were arrested for preaching in the streets and clapped in the Tolbooth. The Society of Friends finally found a meeting house in the Pleasance, away from the persecution of town officials.

The west side of the Pleasance was once the site of the Chirurgeon's Hall. In 1505, the surgeons and barbers were formed into a Corporation by the Town Council, and later Queen Mary exempted them from serving on juries because patients called them out at all hours. In 1657 the surgeons and apothecaries were united into one community and from that time ceased to act as barbers. Their old building on the Pleasance was long a source of comment, for, in addition to the dissecting theatre, they had a museum with a mummy. Another medical event that was associated with the Pleasance was the opening in 1776 of Edinburgh's first public dispensary on West Richmond Street, through the efforts of Dr Andrew Duncan.

85

Edinburgh, a city of wynds and closes, has but one Vennel. It climbs steeply from the Grassmarket, skirts George Heriot's School, and continues to Lauriston Place. It is the best place to see the remnants of the Flodden Wall.

Following the Scottish defeat at Flodden on 9 September 1513, Edinburgh became greatly concerned about the defensive boundaries of the city. The King's Wall was in existence but was not considered a suitable barrier against possible attack by the Auld Enemy. Early in 1514 the Magistrates of the city levied a tax of £5 on each inhabitant and work on the wall was begun. Its construction took many years but the result was formidable. The wall was high and over three feet thick. It had numerous gates and towers and was crenellated and furnished with embrasures and loopholes. In some places it was reinforced with a rampart of earth.

The wall ran from the southern slope of the Castle Rock, along the west side of the Grassmarket and up the eastern side of the Vennel almost to Lauriston, where it turned east to the corner of Teviot Row and proceeded north to the Bristo Port. From there it continued east past the university and Drummond Street to the Pleasance, crossing the Cowgate, and on to the Nether Bow Port. The enclosures was completed by the houses on the west side of St Mary's Wynd. In the Vennel, along with part of the wall, one can see a tower which belonged to the original barrier.

In the eighteenth century some workmen digging by the Vennel tower unearthed five skulls. It was subsequently established that these were the remains of the publicly impaled heads of Covenanters who had been executed in the seventeenth century. Their followers had evidently rescued their remains by night and hidden them in the ground just outside the wall. The relics were given a final resting-place in Greyfriars Kirkyard.

Towards the Lauriston end of the Vennel the numerous turrets, chimneys, and pinnacles of George Heriot's Hospital School come into view. The building is one of the best surviving examples of Scottish Renaissance architecture. One of its most amazing features is the controlled exuberance of its ornamental detail. There are two hundred richly-ornamented windows in the building and no two alike. The building, which opened for thirty boys in 1659, after briefly being commandeered by Cromwell as a hospital, was constructed with funds left by George Heriot, court jeweller to James VI and his consort, Anne of Denmark.

Heriot, often referred to as 'Jingling Geordie', was born in Edinburgh in 1563, the son of a prominent goldsmith. On his marriage at the age of twenty-three the younger Heriot was given a goldsmith's shop by his father. It was located in one of the 'luckenbooths' by St Giles, and here Geordie plied his trade and acted as a moneylender. He soon came to the attention of royalty and was declared official goldsmith to Anne of Denmark. Heriot could not have had a better customer, for not only was the Queen fond of presenting handsome diamond rings to her friends, she also borrowed sums of money frequently from her jeweller. In 1601 Heriot also became the official jeweller to the King, and when James VI and his court moved to London, Heriot followed.

Heriot died on 12 February 1623 and is buried in St Martin-in-the-Fields in London. The major portion of his estate, after bequests to dependents and friends, was left to the Provost, Bailies, Ministers of the Established Church, and the Town Council of Edinburgh, to pay the cost of building the hospital school for the raising and education of fatherless boys and freemason's sons.

87

72. *The Vennel.*

One of Edinburgh's most charming characteristics is the way in which tradition continues to harmonise with the changing modern scene. The Royal Company of Archers, which has been functioning since the seventeenth century, is a part of the city scene as enduring as the One o'Clock Gun.

The Archers were formed in 1676 during the reign of Charles II. The originators were 'an influential body of Noblemen and Gentlemen, who met for the purpose of encouraging the Noble and Useful Recreation of Archery, for many years much neglected'. Prowess with the bow had been at one time much more than a recreation; it was a decisive weapon in the warfare of the Middle Ages, when Scotland was poor and sparsely populated, and always in danger of English attack. In an attempt to raise the standard of Scottish archery, James IV (1406-37) issued a famous statute in which he incidentally forbade any man to play the game of 'futeball', under penalty of a fifty-shilling fine. A similar restriction was put on golf.

The Royal Company of Archers has a seal which bears the figures of Cupid and Mars and the motto: 'In Peace and Warr'. In 1704, Queen Anne granted a Charter which established the Royal Company's right of 'perpetual access to all public butts, plains and pasturages legally allotted for shooting arrows with the bow. . .'. In return for this favour, the Queen and her successors could ask the Archers for 'one pair of barbed arrows' yearly. A reddendo of silver arrows, mounted on a velvet cushion, has been presented on eleven occasions at the request of the Monarch. The first was given to George IV in 1822, and the most recent to the Queen in 1953.

The State visit of George IV in 1822 was an important landmark in the history of the Royal Company of Archers, because for the first time its members were permitted to describe themselves as the 'King's Body Guard for Scotland'. Fifty Archers marched on each side of the royal carriage in the procession from Leith to Holyrood, where the Captain-General and forty other Archers waited to greet the King and attend him throughout his stay in Scotland.

Each year the Archers, in their uniform of dark green, shoot in the Meadows for the Edinburgh Arrow, a trophy presented by the Magistrates of the city in 1709. Their target, called the 'clout', is circular, three feet wide, and stuffed with straw. They shoot at a range of nine score (180 yards). Butt shooting over a short range of 100 feet is practised at the Archers' Hall, their headquarters in Buccleuch Street.

The Meadows have long been a favourite place of recreation, but during the Second World War much of them was given over to allotment gardening. Long ago the area was covered by a loch whose reedy shores were the haunt of innumerable wildfowl and which served as a watering place for the animals of Drumsheugh Forest. The Meadows and the adjacent Bruntsfield Links are all that is left of the wild and lonely Boroughmuir, which stretched as far as the Braid Hills. In the sixteenth century the land on the south shore of the loch was feued by a Cistercian convent, and early in the seventeenth century it was partially drained. During draining operations many animal bones were uncovered, including those of a gigantic stag. In 1722 the land was leased to Thomas Hope of Rankeillor, president of the Honourable Society of Improvers in the Knowledge of Agriculture in Scotland. Hope made great improvements in the area, completely draining the loch, and making a walk lined with lime trees. His name is commemorated in the area known as Hope Park, at the south-east corner of the Meadows.

73. *The Royal Company of Archers, on the Meadows, shooting for the Edinburgh Arrow. The buildings beyond the trees are* (left) *the Simpson Maternity Pavilion, and* (right) *the Royal Infirmary.*

74. *The Canongate Kirk, built in 1688, at a cost of 43,000 merks Scots.*

Before the seventeenth century, residenters in the Canongate used Holyrood Abbey Chapel as their parish kirk. But in 1686 King James VII told the Privy Council that he wanted the Chapel for the Knights of the Thistle. The result was the construction of Canongate Church, and the building was erected with funds originally intended for the rebuilding of a church on Castle Hill. Thomas Moodie was the benefactor and his crest is prominently displayed on the façade.

The design of the kirk is unusual, and the plain, inornate basilica is decorated with a stag's antlers bearing a cross, the insignia of the Burgh of Canongate. This emblem provides a link with Holyrood and is representative of a legend concerning King David I. In 1128, while hunting on a holy day against the orders of the Church, the King was cut off from the rest of his party and confronted by a large white stag, which unhorsed him. A vision of the Cross appeared between the stag's antlers, giving the King courage to chase the animal away. In thanksgiving for his deliverance, the King set up an Abbey in honour of the Holy Rood, St Mary the Virgin and All the Saints.

John Craig (1561) was the first Reformed minister of the Canongate. He later became a colleague of John Knox at St Giles. Craig's successor was John Brand, who published the banns of marriage between Mary, Queen of Scots, and Darnley. Later Brand courageously refused to publish the banns between Mary and Bothwell.

The interior of the kirk was restored in 1950, in a manner which enhanced its inherent simplicity and brought a new atmosphere of airiness and light to its grey walls. Of interest in the church are the Royal Pew and the pew for Edinburgh Castle, both of which denote the Kirk's position as parish church.

As in the Greyfriars, the gravestones in the kirkyard commemorate many prominent names. Scotland's literary and intellectual tradition is particularly well represented. One thinks first of the poet Robert Fergusson, whose monument was erected by Burns, but also of Dugald Stewart, the philosopher, and of Adam Smith, author of *Wealth of Nations*.

Buried here, too, are Hugh William Williams (1773-1829), a landscape painter described by Lord Cockburn as 'by far the most beautiful painter in water-colours in Scotland up to his time' and also believed to have been the originator of the name 'Modern Athens' for Edinburgh; and Sir John Watson Gordon (1788-1864), the portrait-painter, a close friend of Raeburn, and president of the Royal Scottish Academy in 1850. There are also Alexander Runciman (1736-85), a historical painter, one of whose murals is in St Patrick's Roman Catholic Church in the Cowgate, and, in more recent times, the architect Robert Hurd (1905-63), who was so closely associated with the restoration of the Canongate.

Mrs Maclehose (Burns's Clarinda, to whom he wrote 'Ae Fond Kiss') lies in the kirkyard, as does Lord Provost George Drummond, the father of the New Town. Tradition says that the murdered Rizzio, Italian secretary to Mary Queen of Scots, is also buried here in an obscure corner.

James Ballantyne (1772-1833), one of Sir Walter Scott's closest associates, is buried here. It was at Ballantyne's home at 10 St John Street that Scott first read some of the Waverley Novels aloud. Also buried in the kirkyard is Ballantyne's younger brother John (1774-1821), who, though partly responsible for the loss of Scott's fortune, nevertheless remained a close friend of his. At his funeral Scott is said to have whispered to a friend, 'I feel as if there will be less sunshine for me from this day forth'.

75. *Holyrood, Dumbiedykes, Salisbury Crags, Hunter's Bog, and Arthur's Seat.*

IV. HOLYROOD PARK

From certain districts in Edinburgh, notably Newington, Arthur's Seat has the outline of a lion couchant, its head upstanding high, its haunches slightly rising. Others in the city will tell you that it looks more like a sleeping elephant or perhaps a sphinx—the shape depends on the viewpoint. From the air, the distinctive outline loses its identity and one can see, more clearly, the diversity of ground.

Arthur's Seat, at 822 feet, is the highest of the seven hills on which Edinburgh is built. It is most easily climbed by a path near the car-park at Dunsappie Loch. It is also more or less the centre of the 648-acre Holyrood Park, also known as the Queen's or King's Park. A spectacular road called the Queen's Drive, after Queen Victoria, which encircles Arthur's Seat, has been described as the finest carriage-drive in Europe.

Holyrood Park is perhaps most beautiful in spring when the red rocky out-crops are ablaze with the fragrant yellow bloom of the whins. Mary, Queen of Scots, fully appreciated this seasonal event, and in 1564 gave an outdoor engage-ment party for two friends beneath Whinny Hill, when the blooms were at their height. In spring, too, May Day is observed with a sunrise service on the top of Arthur's Seat. The custom may have its origin in a pre-Christian ceremony of sun worship. Today, young maidens attending the service traditionally wash their faces in the morning dew in the hopes of improving their beauty.

According to legend, Arthur's Seat is named after King Arthur who reigned over Strathclyde from 508 to 542 and who was slain at the Battle of Camelon, near Falkirk. In ancient times Arthur's Seat and the surrounding park, which is about five miles in circumference, were within the boundaries of the ancient sanctuary of Holyrood. Here a man could be safe from his creditors for twenty-four hours. It is said that, when the time limit expired, the debtor applied to the Abbey for permission to leave the park without fear of molestation.

The confines of the Park were also a refuge in other circumstances. In 1645, during a severe bout of plague in the city, the sick were segregated and sent to the Park where they were put under the care of a doctor. Many died there and were buried on the spot. Before this time the Park was heavily wooded and a natural haunt for thieves, even though close to the town. In 1728 a hiker in the hills accidentally stumbled on an old hideout of thieves in the Catnick in Salisbury Crags. It was approached from a shallow pit and completely fitted out with dressed skins on the walls. Behind Salisbury Crags lies an area known as Hunter's Bog, near which the Jacobites encamped in 1745.

There are three lochs in Holyrood Park—Duddingston on the south side with its sanctuary for waterfowl; the secluded Dunsappie Loch; and the artificial loch known as St Margaret's, which is especially popular with Edinburgh's children. Above this loch can be seen the ruins of St Anthony's Chapel, erected in the fifteenth century. It is believed that this chapel was connected with the hospital founded by King James I at Leith about 1430 for the treatment of 'St Anthony's Fire', or erysipelas. Not far from the ruin, on the cliff face, is a fissure called St Anthony's Cave, and south of this stands St Anthony's Well.

Throughout the year, flocks of sheep graze the hills, and not only give them a pastoral air, but also help to keep the grass in order.

77. *Auld Reekie.*

The most comprehensive view of Edinburgh and certainly of the Calton Hill can be obtained from Arthur's Seat. On top of the Calton Hill, which stands just east of Princes Street, are perched an odd assortment of structures. The slender column is a memorial to Lord Nelson, the victor of Trafalgar, and is shaped to represent that great English admiral's telescope. A few yards away stands the National Monument, which can still occasionally cause Edinburgh people some embarrassment, when they overhear visitors speculating about the 'ruin'.

In 1822 it was decided to build on this spot a memorial to commemorate the outstanding achievements of the Scottish soldiers in the Napoleonic Wars. Edinburgh was then enjoying its neo-Greek phase in architecture, which had earned it the name of Athens of the North; and Playfair was commissioned to design a monument which would take the form of the Parthenon. The foundation stone was laid on 27 August 1822, with great ceremony and amid canon salutes from the Castle, Salisbury Crags, and Leith Fort. Unfortunately funds ran out before the structure was half completed—a misfortune which gave the unfinished monument the tag of 'Edinburgh's Folly' or 'Scotland's Pride and Poverty'. For many people, however, the truncated monument is more arresting, and also perhaps more truly symbolic of its theme.

95

76. *The Calton Hill, from Arthur's Seat.*

78, 79. *Autumn and Winter, in the Queen's Park.*

Winter snow, filling a thousand crevices, softens the deeply etched face of Salisbury Crags, but serves only to emphasise the line of the adventurous track known with affection as the Radical Road.

Before the Radical Road was constructed in 1820, a rough path wound around the base of the Crags. Here, of a morning or evening, David Hume, Boswell, and Sir Walter Scott often strolled, pensively planning new projects. Scott, in fact, had a hand in the construction of the new road, for it was at his suggestion that a group of private citizens banded together to employ some unemployed weavers from the West of Scotland to improve the pathway. The weavers were at odds with the prevailing political climate; and so it was called the 'Radical Road'.

When the road was finished it was proposed that Samson's Ribs nearby should be transformed into a show garden, with rare heaths from the Cape of Good Hope and other foreign parts, and that the existing pathways be extended to aid walkers. The Earl of Haddington, then Hereditary Keeper of the Royal Park, opposed this suggestion on the grounds that the grazing flocks of sheep would be disturbed. Lord Haddington, however, soon roused public indignation by reopening the quarries at Salisbury Crags and selling the stone to pave the streets of London. In 1843, the rights of the park were purchased for £40,000 and handed over to the Commissioners of Woods and Forest, thus putting an end to the commercial disintegration of the Crags.

80. *The Castle, St Leonard's Bank, and the Kaimheid.*

The visit of George IV to Edinburgh, in 1822, was an event of great import. No British king had been within the walls of Holyrood Palace for nearly a hundred and fifty years, and great preparations were made for the royal party. It is believed that the visit itself was undertaken on the suggestion of Sir Walter Scott. Certainly, Scott had a major role in planning the elaborate receptions and processions which kept the Monarch occupied for a whole fortnight.

The King landed at Leith and drove through gay streets to Holyrood while salutes boomed from the Castle. Though Holyrood was the ceremonial starting-point each day of the King's formal activities, he resided at Dalkeith House as the guest of the Duke of Buccleuch. Only a few functions were held within the Palace, a throne room having been hastily constructed before the King's arrival.

81. 'The Arrival of HIS MOST GRACIOUS MAJESTY GEORGE IV at his ancient PALACE of HOLYROOD on the 16 of Augt. 1822'. *Coloured engraving, 37·5 × 56·2 cm., painted and engraved by W. Turner de Lond. Dedicated* 'To the Right Honble. Sir William Arbuthnot Bart., Lord Provost of EDINBURGH, the constituted Authorities, Military, Celtic Society, Highland Chiefs, Royal Compy. of Archers &c.' *Central Public Library Edinburgh. In this deceptively pompous picture, Holyrood strongly resembles the Bastille, and the King himself can scarcely be seen.*

82. *General View of Edinburgh, from Arthur's Seat. Watercolour 36·2 ×
51·3 cm., by J. W. Williams, 1829. Huntly House Museum, Edinburgh.*

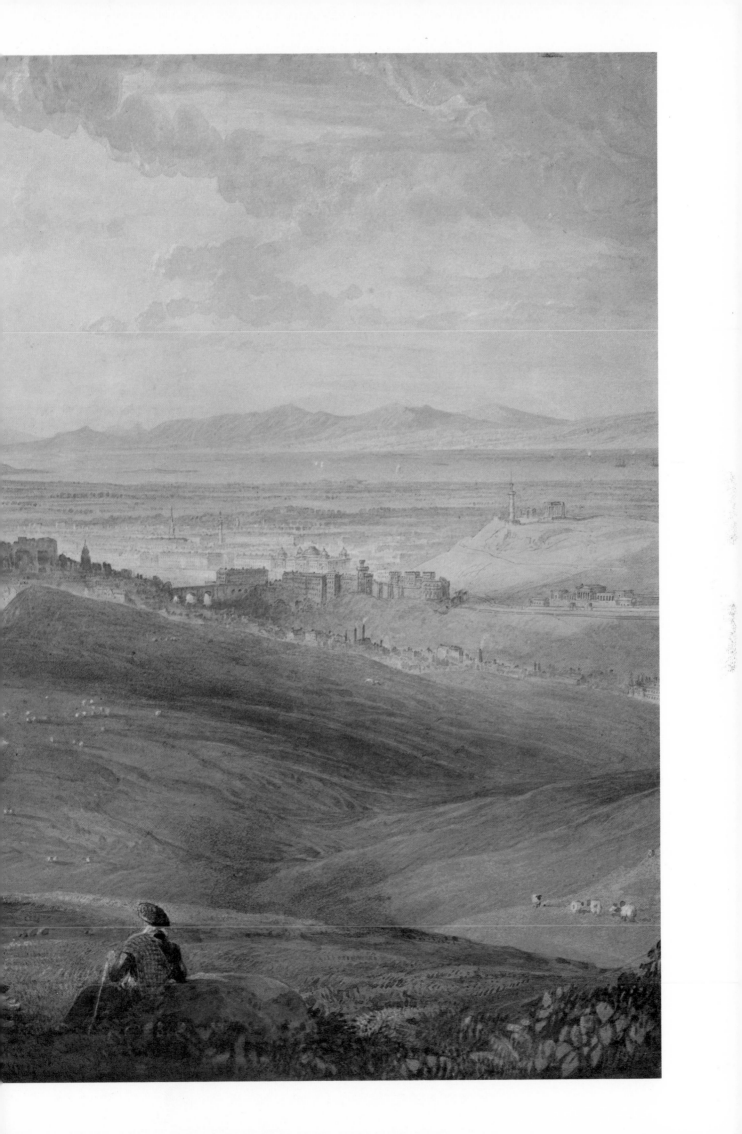

83. 'High Street, from Fountainwell'. *Engraving (hand-coloured),*
8·9 × 12·5 cm., drawn by J. Ewbank, engraved by W. H. Lizars,
c. 1825. Central Public Library, Edinburgh.

84. 'St Mary's Wynd, from the Pleasance'. *Engraving (hand-coloured),*
9·4 × 14·7 cm., drawn by T. M. Shepherd, engraved by J. B. Allan,
c. 1825. Oliver & Boyd Ltd, Tweeddale Court.

Landscape-painting in Scotland developed in the early eighteenth century under the influence of Italian and Dutch artists, whose engravings and prints had strayed here from the Continent. James Norie (1684-1757), an Edinburgh house-painter who decorated chimney pieces and door lintels with classical scenes, was one of the first to venture into this new medium. Previously the public taste had been entirely for portrait-painting. Norie's works were liberally scattered with Roman ruins, arches, and temples, and members of his family continued this decorative tradition. The real impetus in landscape-painting, however, was provided by Alexander Nasmyth (1758-1840).

Nasmyth had been apprenticed to his architect father (who played a major role in the design of George Square), but the young man soon showed an aptitude for painting and was allowed to pursue this interest. He studied in Edinburgh at the Trustees' Academy under Alexander Runciman, and in London under Allan Ramsay. In 1782 he went to Rome for two years, finally returning to Edinburgh to set up a studio in St James's Square. Here in 1787 he painted a portrait of Robert Burns. Nasmyth's conversion to landscape-painting was particularly fortunate for Edinburgh, for the city was immortalised in views from Calton Hill and the Mound. Nasmyth was also influential in the field of architecture, one of his designs being St Bernard's Well.

Until Hugh William Williams (1773-1829) emerged as a landscape-painter, painting of this kind had been done from memory. But Williams was one who insisted on a more realistic representation, and many of his water colour sketches, in fact, bear the words 'coloured on the spot'. His view from Arthur's Seat, with its classical composition and strict attention to detail, justifies his title 'Grecian' Williams. It is believed that this picture was executed just before his death, because it shows the Royal High School (1829).

Williams was Welsh, but was born aboard his father's ship during a voyage to the West Indies. His parents died when he was very young, and he was brought up by his grandmother and her second husband, an Italian, who discovered the boy's talent for drawing. Williams spent his professional life in Edinburgh, with the exception of trips to Greece and Italy. In 1820 he published *Travels in Italy, Greece and the Ionian Islands*. Few of Williams's works were done in oils, for he preferred to work in broad washes. This preference gives a relatively modern look to his work.

One of many painters attracted to Edinburgh during this period of development in landscape painting was John Ewbank (1799-1847) of Newcastle. Ewbank's print of the High Street from the Fountain Well, engraved by the accomplished engraver, William Home Lizars (1788-1859), exhibits the former's supreme sense of composition. Ewbank, one of the first members of the Royal Scottish Academy, displayed his true talent in the painting of seascapes and ships. The feeling for light in his maritime pictures contrasts sharply with his work ashore, where his colours often seem a little too heavy.

Lizars, the engraver, was a man whose early artistic ambitions were thwarted by the untimely death of his father. Left with the responsibility of his mother and a family to support, he had to forfeit painting for engraving. It is believed that Lizars' own capabilities as a painter—his *Reading the Will* and *A Scotch Wedding* were exhibited at the Royal Academy in London in 1812—would have carried him far had he been allowed to develop them.

103

85. *The Castle, Tolbooth St John's, and St Giles, from the Radical Road. The dome beneath Tolbooth St John's is that of the Old College.*

86. *Holland House, one of the University's new halls of residence, from Samson's Ribs.*

Named after a recent Principal of the University, Holland House stands on the Dalkeith Road, with Arthur's Seat and some open land to the back of it.

In the nineteenth century Edinburgh University students either lived in lodgings in the city or at home with their parents. In the early years of this century, however, some tentative moves were made to accommodate junior members of the University in various hostels where they could lead a communal life.

After the end of the Second World War, the building of hostels became a part of the major general plan of University extension to the south. Holland House, one of the first of these new developments, houses a hundred and fifty male students in circumstances often of greater comfort than those obtaining in the ancient colleges of Oxford and Cambridge.

Admirable though the building of these hostels is, from the University point of view, they can also play their part in the civic life of Edinburgh. Town and Gown work harmoniously together, and the use of hostels during vacation times is an example.

Edinburgh has recently been discovering her capital status as host to international conferences; and, especially during the summer vacation, such buildings as Holland House have solved the problem of providing suitable accommodation.

87. *The Royal Gateway to the Palace of Holyrood House.*

88. *The Palace and Palace Yard. The oldest part of the Palace is James IV's tower* (left).

There has been a Palace of Holyroodhouse since about 1501, though only the northwest tower remains of the original building constructed by James IV. The building was damaged by fire during an English invasion in 1543, and again in 1650 shortly after Cromwell had quartered his troops there. Cromwell had the palace rebuilt, but when Charles II was restored to the throne, Cromwell's work was pulled down and Bruce of Balcaskie was appointed architect. The present building, with its distinctive Franco-Scottish style, is his work.

The building-accounts for the years 1674-8 give an impressive idea of the work—stone from quarries in Fife and South Queensferry; marble mantlepieces from Italy; timber and tiles from Holland; and glass from France. A Dutch artist, Jacobus de Wet or James de Witt, was employed to paint portraits of all the Scottish kings for the Picture Gallery—a fact which has prompted much comment, since the 110 works were completed in two years and are of kings both real and legendary, from 'Fergus I, B.C. 330', to James VI (1566-1625).

89. *The Castle, Princes Street, and George Street, and* (in foreground) *the Calton Hill.*

90. *The New Town, bounded* (left) *by Queen Street and* (right) *by Princes Street, and bisected by George Street. Charlotte Square* (foreground) *is balanced against St Andrew Square* (at the far end of George Street).

V. PRINCES STREET

James Craig's plan for the original New Town, stretching north from the Nor' Loch Valley, still remains an example of inspired town planning.

Formally approved by the Town Council in 1767, Craig's plan was simple yet strikingly effective in execution, one of its principal merits being its self-containment. George Street was the main thoroughfare, with the ends closed by squares and churches dedicated to St Andrew and St George. Unfortunately this part of the scheme was thwarted by Sir Lawrence Dundas, who owned property at the east end and wanted his town house placed in the position intended for the church. He got his way. His town house is now occupied by the Royal Bank of Scotland, and the St Andrew's Church is in George Street. The plateau on which the New Town was to sit had a natural hollow to the east, now crossed by Waterloo Bridge; and, on the west end, it abutted the property of the Earl of Moray. Craig therefore gave his scheme these limits, with no east or west exit from either St Andrew Square or Charlotte Square (originally called St George's Square). Crossing the main axis of George Street were Castle Street, Frederick Street and Hanover Street. Each of the eight blocks was divided by a side street parallel to George Street. Later generations have unfortunately not adhered to the original building code.

Envy the traveller whose first glimpse of Edinburgh is to the west—coming up from the depths of Waverley Station, into the bright sunlight, with the panorama of the Castle, the Mound and Princes Street spread before him. This is the classic view of the city—and one which is unequalled anywhere in the world.

Over the years sporadic attempts were made to alter this view by building along the south side of Princes Street, and levelling the gardens. Fortunately, public-spirited citizens invariably appeared at the right time to block these well-meant but devastating projects. In a famous open letter to the Lord Provost, Lord Cockburn ironically expounded the 'Best Ways of Spoiling the Beauty of Edinburgh'. Chief among these was what Cockburn called 'the absolutely insane project' of building along the south side of Princes Street. Happily, Cockburn found allies in a group of advocates; and a statute was passed, which prohibited the closing up of Princes Street. Of this struggle Cockburn wrote feelingly: 'Those who remember the battle, have scarcely drawn their breath freely since'.

Cockburn wrote, too, of the presence of the railway in the valley between the Castle and the New Town, calling it a 'lamentable and irreparable blunder'. Many today echo his sentiments, for its presence in the heart of the city is still a subject of controversy, despite its practical value. Waverley Station, however, had become almost an institution in its own right. Though built in the nineteenth century, it remains one of the largest railway stations in the world, covering an area of about 25 acres, most of it under glass.

As in many cities, the impetus for bringing the railway to Edinburgh was the developing demand for coal. As early as 1817, a committee of Lothian landowners asked Robert Stevenson, the lighthouse engineer, to make a survey of possible railway routes. Stevenson mapped three different routes, proposing a terminus in the East Meadows. Of the three routes, the one most feasible ran by way of Abbeyhill and Piershill Barracks to Northfield and Duddingston Mills, then proceeded to what is now New Craighall, Monktonhall, and across the River Esk to Dalkeith. Stevenson's plan, of course, was based on horse-drawn wagons, easy gradients, and cast-iron rails which were only four feet long and laid on stone blocks. He hoped to build the whole main line for £50,000 and reduce cartage costs from one shilling to sixpence a mile. Ten years after Stevenson's initial survey, a company of subscribers made another survey of the proposed Edinburgh to Dalkeith railway. This line, as it was finally built, started from St Leonard's and ran to Newcraighall, Millerhill, Sheriffhall Crossroads, Eskbank, and Dalhousie Mains to Dalkeith.

Between 1836 and 1846, the country went railway mad and in one year there were more than three hundred railway bills before Parliament. In 1836 George Stevenson carried out another survey—this time for the Edinburgh and Dunbar Railway Company. He selected the spot where the Waverley Station now stands as being the most suitable for connexion with the railways to Leith and Glasgow, which were then being built. Before this time, the area beneath the North Bridge had been set aside as a fruit and vegetable market, but with the laying of track through Princes Street Gardens in 1847, the market was moved to the east side of the North Bridge. There it remained for some years, finally being succeeded by the building of Waverley Market in 1869. Today the Market is used primarily as an exhibition hall with dog, flower and trade shows being held there at regular intervals.

91. *The Castle, National Gallery, Royal Scottish Academy, Scott Monument, and Princes Street, from the North British Hotel.*

92. *One of Edinburgh's most dramatic views: the Royal Scottish Academy, New College, Tolbooth St John's, and Patrick Geddes's Outlook Tower, from the foot of Hanover Street.*

93. *Part of the Old Town, from the Mound.*

Hanover Street naturally conjures up thoughts of Germanic influence, and the name does, in fact, spring from the Hanoverian associations of the royal family. George III (1760-1820) took a close interest in the building of the first New Town and brought his influence to bear on the important issue of naming the streets. Princes Street was called St Giles Street in the original plan of the New Town, but the King objected, and so it was named after the King's sons. George Street was named after the King, and Queen Street after his consort, Charlotte of Mecklenburg-Strelitz. Frederick Street was named after the King's second son. His fifth son, Ernest, carried the title of Duke of Cumberland and King of Hanover.

Because of its junction with the foot of the Mound, Hanover Street has always been the busiest of the northern tributaries from Princes Street. In its early days the commercial enterprises in Hanover Street included a lapidary, a lace and muslin printer, a combmaker, a perfumer, a staymaker, and a brass-founder. These tradesmen mingled happily with the gentry, who had built their houses along the street. Among them, at No. 33, was Lord Meadowbank, who had been known at the Bar, until 1792, as Allan Maconochie; at No. 39, Marjoribanks of Marjoribanks; and at No. 54, Sir John Graham Dalyell, who published *Scottish Poems of the Sixteenth Century* and *Bannatyne Memorials*. The Merchants Hall at No. 14 was formerly the premises of the City of Glasgow Bank.

Princes Street is many things to many people. It is a good place to view the passing scene and to catch the essence of the city, both domestic and international —the advocates with black hats and rolled umbrellas striding up the Mound; the housewives with large shopping bags looking for bargains in the chain stores; blond Scandinavians in pink trousers; Breton sailors with red pompoms on their caps; children eating ice cream and feeding pigeons in the Gardens, and an occasional soldier in tartan trews; Americans with cameras round their necks, and schoolboys with dark jackets and bags on their backs; office boys out for a lunchtime stroll and teenage girls in the newest mod fashion, giggling in groups of three—everywhere people of every age, description, and nationality stravaiguing on one of the world's most famous thoroughfares. It seems natural that nearly all of the city's bus-routes should touch Princes Street—it is so obviously a nucleus.

The entertainment value of the Street is manifold. In an active mood, one can stroll, putter in hand, round the eighteen-hole putting green in East Princes Street Gardens, or undertake the demanding climb to the top of the Scott Monument. For pure spectating Princes Street has no equal, two possible enjoyments being the Floral Clock and the Speakers' Corner just east of the Royal Scottish Academy. And, just when the abundance of activity has dulled the senses, the One o'Clock Gun sharply charges the air, and clears the mind.

Princes Street has been the scene of many famous and historic parades, shows, and processions. One yearly event which particularly pleases the younger citizens is the fireworks display at the time of the International Festival. Of the many royal visits, the most spectacular in recent years was that of King Olav of Norway, who in 1962 became the first foreign monarch to make a state visit to Scotland. The street was colourfully decorated for the occasion; and Edinburgh people, who are sometimes accused of being indifferent, turned out in their thousands. Crush barriers and railings erected along the street held back the crowds as they watched King Olav ride in procession from Princes Street Station in a state landau.

An equally spectacular event—though of a different nature—took place on Princes Street on 18 August 1951. The event as advertised was a March of a Thousand Pipers—*The Scotsman* later summed it up, in a headline, as CHAOS IN PRINCES STREET. The march, which took place the day before the opening of the International Festival, preceded a Gathering of the Clans and Highland Games at Murrayfield. The pipers were scheduled to march down the Mound and turn west into Princes Street, marching sixteen abreast. In the event, the pipers were fortunate to be able to march eight abreast, for an estimated half-a-million people turned out. A *Scotsman* reporter who viewed the scene from the tower of St John's Episcopal Church at the West End described the march as 'a rich mosaic of colour weaving its way through a tumultuous mass of people'. His wasn't the only vantage-point, for he wrote of the Castle as being 'clothed' with people. Those on the ground were less fortunate in their viewpoint. When it became obvious that the pavements were fully lined, the people stood under the old tram standards in the middle of Princes Street, and finally in the street itself. As *The Scotsman* reporter observed, 'At times it appeared as if the crowds on both sides of the street would converge completely. As it was, there was only a narrow strip left. . .'. But through this narrow strip marched the pipers, led by a 70-year-old drum major, John Seton, of Dunoon. Miraculously, in all this teeming humanity there were no serious injuries.

94. *At the Mound.*

95. *St John's Episcopal Church, from the promenade in West Princes Street Gardens.*

To the spectator standing towards the western end of Princes Street, the Castle Rock is dominated by a stately building in the baronial style. This is the old Castle hospital. Its ugly neighbour, the Barracks, towers over the southern side and mercifully is out of sight from Princes Street. Barrack stores arose on these sites about 1755, but were reconstructed in their present form in the late nineteenth century. The Castle's first hospital in modern times was the Great Hall, from the Crimean War until 1888. The present hospital building was used in this capacity during the Second World War but is now an Army pay office.

Edinburgh Castle no longer has a garrison stationed within its walls, though a small detachment is on guard-duty at the gates. Nowadays the Castle accommodates the offices of the Rear Headquarters, Scottish Command. This, of course, was not always so. In *Memorials of the Castle* (1850), James Grant says that in 1684, the garrison included two drummers, a chaplain, a 'chyrurgeon', a scrivener, and 108 'centinels', and that in his own day the Castle had room for 3,000 infantry.

96. *The Castle, from West Princes Street Gardens.*

98. *New College, from East Princes Street Gardens.*

In Scotland, the diminutive of a man's name or calling is often a sign of affectionate respect—thus 'postie' for postman. Similarly street orderlies, once called scavengers, are still affectionately called 'scaffies'.

When the entire population of Edinburgh lived along the Castle ridge in the Old Town, the link-boys who delivered messages and carried water up the winding stairs of the tenements were called 'caddies'—the word being the Scottish adaptation of the French *cadet*. Nowadays, of course, caddies still carry golf-clubs. In the speech of Edinburgh's children, the wardens of the city's many parks are usually 'parkies', and the small sweet-shops of the back-streets may also have a syllable added—becoming 'shoppies'. For that matter, Scottish children often call the sugary confections within the shoppie 'sweeties'. One other term of address, which often startles strangers, is 'Hen'. Ladies so addressed need not take offence, for none is intended. One might call it the Scots equivalent of the Cockney 'Luv'.

119

97. *Princes Street.*

For many, the romanticism of Edinburgh is best appreciated at night, after rainfall, when the street lights bounce a million reflexions off the wet paving stones. Others prefer the sharp etching produced by a snowfall—the soft white clinging to the vertical lines of buildings, bestowing on them additional height. Because of Edinburgh's proximity to the sea, anything more than a powdering of snow is almost a rarity. A snowfall, especially when followed by sunshine, gives the city a new personality; for example, the Castle seen from St Cuthbert's Churchyard almost takes on the fine quality of an Oriental silk screen.

Most kirkyards in Scotland are notable for their trimness and care—and the well-cared-for grounds of St Cuthbert's are a surprisingly secluded oasis at the bustling crossroads of the West End. With the exception of St Margaret's Chapel, in the Castle, St Cuthbert's is the oldest religious building in Edinburgh. In all probability it was founded by Malcolm Canmore (1058-93) and his Queen, Margaret. Until the building of the New Town, it was, of course, an outpost of Edinburgh—its position marking the western end of the Nor' Loch. The present church contains nothing of the original medieval structure. A tower dating from 1789 is incorporated in the existing edifice, which was rebuilt in 1892-3 in an Italian Renaissance style. The church bells are among the most familiar sounds of Edinburgh.

Among the celebrated men buried in St Cuthbert's churchyard are Alexander Napier of Merchiston, inventor of logarithms, and Thomas de Quincey, author of *The Opium Eater*. At the south-west corner of the graveyard stands a stout stone tower, with blocked-up windows, bearing the date 1827. Like everything built in Edinburgh at that time, it was obviously meant to last. This was a watch-tower against the body-snatchers. It is difficult to believe that a famous churchyard at the west end of Princes Street could have been vulnerable to this danger while the great expansion of the New Town was going on round about, but the existence of the tower indicates the panic, on this subject, that infected the times.

North of St Cuthbert's, and on the corner of Lothian Road and Princes Street, stands St John's Episcopal Church, which was erected in 1817. The architect was William Burn and the style is modern Gothic after St George's Chapel, Windsor. The original church had a tower with an open lantern on the top, but during a wind storm in 1818 the tower broke through the roof and floor, causing great damage. The small cemetery south of the church, with ornamental vaults, is the burial place of Sir Henry Raeburn, the painter; James Donaldson, the founder of Donaldson's hospital; and Catherine Sinclair, the novelist.

Across the road from St John's is the towering red block of the Caledonian Hotel. At the rear of the hotel used to be located Princes Street Station, popularly known as the 'Caley', the former terminus of the West Coast railway route from England. This station was declared superfluous following the Beeching Report, and closed in September 1965. The station, completed in 1893, was the last of three built in this vicinity by the Caledonian Railway Company. The first, intended to be a magnificent colonnaded building of Italian style, was only partially constructed before the railway ran short of funds. The remains of this station were incorporated in the goods station in Lothian Road. The last of the three stations had a distinctive style, originally, featuring three handsome archways and a semi-domed roof. The Caledonian Hotel was built on top of it in the early twentieth century.

99. *The Castle, in winter, from St Cuthbert's Kirkyard.*

100 (on next two pages). *Princes Street, from the Scott Monument.*

101. *The portico of the Royal Scottish Academy, on the Mound, is one of Edinburgh's most popular trysting-places.*

For close on a century and a half, the art galleries of Edinburgh have made a significant contribution to the culture of the city, and indeed, of Scotland.

The most familiar of these institutions is the Royal Scottish Academy, a massive Greek temple at the foot of the Mound with a stately sculpture of young Queen Victoria on the roof. Since its origin in 1826, the R.S.A. has championed the development of a national and individual school of painting in Scotland. The works of contemporary artists are exhibited in the annual show of the Academy, and the galleries are also made available for exhibitions during the International Festival and for the display of works by other artistic societies. Additionally the Academy administers many charitable funds and prizes.

Behind the R.S.A. stands the National Gallery of Scotland, which like its neighbour was designed by W. H. Playfair. The National Gallery opened in 1859 with a collection of 331 pictures and sculptures. These included Van Dyck's *St Sebastian*, Tiepolo's *Finding of Moses*, and Bassano's *Adoration of the Kings*. In the first seven months the collection drew 80,000 people. It proved so popular that gas lighting was installed in order that the Gallery could remain open in the evening.

By far the most valuable gift ever given to the National Gallery was the bequest made by Mr Alexander Maitland in 1960 in memory of his wife. The twenty-one pictures in the collection, collected over a period of forty-five years, include works by Cézanne, Gauguin, Van Gogh, Degas, Renoir, Modigliani, and Sisley. Since 1946 the Gallery has had, on extended loan, thirty-one paintings from the collection of the Earl of Ellesmere. These include four Titians, four Rembrandts, and several Raphaels.

The Scottish National Portrait Gallery, at the east end of Queen Street, has an interesting history. In 1882 an anonymous Edinburgh citizen offered £10,000 towards the purchase of a collection of national portraits on condition that the Treasury subscribed an equal amount. Later, the same individual offered £20,000 towards a building to house the portrait gallery and the museum of the Society of Antiquaries. Seven years later the donor was revealed as John Ritchie Findlay, owner of *The Scotsman*. Findlay eventually gave £70,000 to the establishment of the Scottish National Portrait Gallery, which includes fine portraits of such famous Scots as Knox, Claverhouse, Napier, Boswell, and Hume.

The red sandstone building, which the Portrait Gallery shares with the National Museum of Antiquities, was designed by Sir Rowand Anderson. The ornamental niches of the exterior are filled with statues of illustrious Scots, notably Mary, Queen of Scots; King James I (1394-1437); the poet, John Barbour; the lawyer, Viscount Stair (1619-95); and Bishop Gavin Douglas (1474-1522). The interior of the central hall is illustrated with murals by William Hole, R.S.A., which depict important events in Scottish history.

The newest of the city's national galleries—that of modern art—was opened in 1960 in Inverleith House, a fine old stone mansion situated in the centre of the Royal Botanic Garden. The art collection comprises paintings, sculpture, drawings and prints from about 1900, and the Scottish artists represented include Pryde, Hunter, Peploe, and Cadell. Also in the exhibition is a Paul Klee drawing, *Snowstorm*; an Edward Wadsworth oil, *Composition, Crank and Chain*; and a Graham Sutherland gouache, *Thistles and Sun*. The house was built in 1747, for James Rocheid of Inverleith, and for many years was the residence of the Regius Keeper of the Botanic Garden.

102. *The polisman, on point duty, in Princes Street.*

103. *The Bank of Scotland, St Giles, New College, Tolbooth St John's, the Outlook Tower, and Allan Ramsay's house, from West Princes Street Gardens.*

New College, with its twin spires staring imperiously down the Mound, was founded after the Disruption within the established church in 1843. Four theology professors were among the breakaway Free Church, and they formed the basis of the faculty of the first theological college of the new Church, at 80 George Street. The Rev. Dr Thomas Chalmers was Principal. Three years later the foundation stone was laid for the college's quarters on the Mound. The architect was W. H. Playfair and initial funds of £21,000 for the building were subscribed by 20 friends of the Church. Since 1936 the adjoining High Church has been the College Library. Today New College is the largest post-graduate theological college in Scotland; and, although it is primarily a training ground for Church of Scotland ministers, a large percentage of its students come from abroad.

Edinburgh has long been noted for its numerous monuments and memorial sculptures, many of the best known being situated in Princes Street Gardens. The newest is the Royal Scots Monument just below the Floral Clock. Designed by Sir Frank Mears, the monument features seven monoliths of sandy pink freestone with carved figures symbolising various phases in the history of the regiment. It was dedicated in 1952. Not far to the west is the prominent equestrian monument to the Royal Scots Greys who fell in the South African War (1899-1902). Rider and horse are one-third larger than life-size and stand on a rocky pedestal.

Elsewhere in West Princes Street Gardens can be seen the benign figure of the poet Allan Ramsay (1686-1758) standing guard over the Floral Clock, and the bronze statue of Sir James Young Simpson (1811-70), physician, the first to use chloroform. The most evocative statue is undoubtedly the centrepiece of the Scottish American Memorial, where a young kilted soldier gazes eternally towards the Castle Rock. The Memorial, raised by Americans to Scots who died in the First World War, was designed by Professor R. Tait McKenzie in 1927.

104. *The Scots Grey, in West Princes Street Gardens.*

105. *Randolph Crescent, Ainslie Place, and Moray Place, with the Water of Leith* (left), *and Leith* (top right).

106. *Moray Place.*

VI. THE NEW TOWN

The original New Town, bounded by Queen Street and Princes Street, was extended several times during the Georgian period. One of these extensions was planned by Gillespie Graham of Orchil in 1822.

Graham had an unusual site with which to work—the hilly and wooded estate belonging to the 10th Earl of Moray's Mansion of Drumsheugh. The most remarkable aspect of this land was the vista it afforded over the valley of the Water of Leith. Graham, however, chose to ignore what another architect might have emphasised; and, instead, designed a pattern consisting of a crescent, an oval and a polygon linked by short streets—the full impact of which really can be appreciated only from the air. The main axis of the design was at an angle of forty-five degrees to Craig's first New Town; and the two plans, when completed, were easily linked. Many of the Moray family names were given to Graham's scheme—the impressive polygon being named after Lord Moray himself. Doune Terrace, one of the connecting streets off Moray Place, was named after Moray's eldest son; and the oval, Ainslie Place, after his second wife. One of the Earl's family's names was conferred on Great Stuart Street, the connecting link between Randolph Crescent and Ainslie Place.

107. *Albyn Place.*

One of the streets built as a connecting link between Moray Place and the New Town designed by James Craig was Albyn Place, which sweeps up to the imposing terrace of Queen Street.

The pilasters and half-columns which adorn both Moray Place and Albyn Place are another example of the Grecian ardour which swept Edinburgh during this period. The developers of the New Town had no access to marble, but they were fortunate in having, at close hand, the calciferous sandstone from the quarries of Craigleith, Barnton, Ravelston, and Hailes. Most of the paving stones for the streets came from Hailes Quarry, while building blocks came from the other three. The quarry of Craigleith was particularly popular, and in addition to helping to supply the needs of the New Town, it also sent stone south, where it was used to build the British Museum and part of Buckingham Palace.

130

108. *Abercromby Place.*

Abercromby Place is a prominent feature of the second New Town designed in 1804 by Robert Reid and William Sibbald. It was the first street in Edinburgh to be constructed in the form of a curve; and people from all parts of the city came to look at this striking architectural development.

The second New Town was established on the slope below the green boundary of Queen Street Gardens. With its main east-west axis of Great King Street, it was intended to be a near-replica of Craig's original plan. Craig, however, had based his scheme on a natural ridge—George Street—and the different land contours in the Reid-Sibbald plan made modifications inevitable.

Both New Towns, however, did have one thing in common—open spaces at each end of the main axis, Drummond Place and Royal Circus being the termination of the Reid-Sibbald plan.

131

109. *St Colme Street.*

Many who walk down North Charlotte Street are mystified by a memorial which, at first glance, seems a miniature Scott Monument. In reality, it was erected to Catherine Sinclair (1800-64), one of Scott's literary friends.

Miss Sinclair was a writer of merit, whose *Holiday House* became a standard children's book. She was a member of the famed Abbotsford circle and delighted in baiting its chief member, Sir Walter. Allegedly, while all Edinburgh was trying to guess the identity of the author of the Waverley Novels, Miss Sinclair handed Scott a portrait, the face draped in muslin, and labelled 'The Great Unknown'. Scott lifted the cloth, saw himself, and smiled, but said nothing. Miss Sinclair was best known for her many charitable works. She erected Edinburgh's first drinking fountain for horses and drivers and introduced cooking depots or soup kitchens for working men, where dinner cost 3d.

132

110. *St Stephen's, at the foot of St Vincent Street.*

Close to the village of Stockbridge, which straddles the Water of Leith, is one of the New Town's most unusual buildings, St Stephen's Church. Built about 1828 to the design of W. H. Playfair, the church stands at the bottom of a steep hill with the street dividing on either side. The body of the church is a square, set diagonally behind the imposing tower, while the interior is octagonal in shape.

St Vincent Street, like several other streets in the area, was named after one of England's famous admirals. The church, which is its most prominent feature, borders the former Silvermills district. Here, according to legend, was erected in the early seventeenth century, a silver mill called 'God's Blessing'. Its high productivity so interested the King that he forced the owner to sell for £5,000. For some reason, the legend concludes, 'God's Blessing' under royal ownership never produced as much silver as before.

133

III. *St George's, Charlotte Square.*

112. *Forres Street.*

One outstanding feature of the New Town is the green copper dome of St George's Church on the west side of Charlotte Square.

Craig's plan for the first New Town proposed a church on this site, terminating the vista from George Street. When Robert Adam prepared his design for Charlotte Square in 1791 he also drew sketches for the church; however, with his death a year later his plan for the church was discarded as too costly. Robert Reid was ultimately appointed architect, and his substitute plan was put into execution between 1811 and 1814. Reid's great Ionic columns at the church entrance have been criticised as being out of proportion with the remainder of the square; but his dome, modelled after St Paul's, compensates for this questionable defect. The church, its congregation long merged with that of St Andrew's, George Street, is now owned by the Corporation.

135

Queen Street, in its infancy, was a popular residential quarter—away from the bustle of Princes Street and with an outlook over the gardens towards the Firth of Forth and the distant shore of Fife. The street was extended east, under the name of York Place, about 1786; and in 1795 Raeburn established his studio at No. 32.

This terraced street, because of its distinguished residents, saw many famous visitors. During his visit to the city in 1884, Robert Browning lunched with the fellows of the Royal College of Physicians at No. 9 and 10 Queen Street. In 1848 Frederic Chopin conducted a *soirée musicale* in the Hopetoun Rooms at No. 72. To this street, too, came the mourners of Sir James Young Simpson, who died in 1870, at No. 52. Simpson's funeral cortège was so long that it took thirty-three minutes to pass. It was fitting homage to a man who came to Edinburgh as a penniless student and stayed to become a world-famous physician. Allegedly, in his Queen Street home, he first discovered the anaesthetic properties of chloroform. One story relates that Simpson poured chloroform on three handkerchiefs—one for himself and the others for two doctors, Keith and Duncan. Simpson was awakened from the effects of his dose by the snoring of Dr Duncan and the thrashing-about of Dr Keith. Nowadays, many of the doors in Queen Street are ornamented with the brass name plates of Writers to the Signet, solicitors, chartered accountants, architects, and stockbrokers.

114. *An address in the New Town of Edinburgh.*

113. *Queen Street, in the afternoon.*

115. *The north side of Charlotte Square, in winter.*

Many in Edinburgh look to Charlotte Square for the first signs of spring. Then the garden is carpeted with crocuses and snowdrops and the returning sun gives warmth to the stone façades. However, it takes winter conditions to point up the magnificence of the architecture—especially Robert Adam's north side. Then, there are no leafy trees to obstruct the view, and distract from the effect of one of Europe's most graceful examples of neo-classical design.

The architects who participated in planning the New Town designed each street as a whole unit with houses an integral part. The removal of even one house from Charlotte Square, Great King Street, or Moray Place would have a ruinous effect. As it is, the addition of dormer windows and plate glass panes and, in some cases, extra doors, has taken the keen edge of perfection from many buildings. Charlotte Square, however, and especially the north side, has been jealously guarded from any such depredation.

The gardens of Charlotte Square are private and were laid out in 1796, though construction of the square was not finally completed until about 1820. In the centre is an equestrian statue of Prince Albert, consort of Queen Victoria. In its early years, the square was known as Edinburgh's Harley Street, because so many physicians stayed there—including Lister, the pioneer in antiseptic surgery, who resided at No. 9 from 1870 to 1877. Earl Haig of Bemersyde, Commander-in-Chief of the British Expeditionary Forces, 1915-19, was born at No. 24.

One of the inspirations in the planning of the New Town was the wide thoroughfares which separated and emphasised the stately Georgian architecture. In the twentieth century, such streets as George Street and Queen Street are now coping with traffic of a density inconceivable to the Georgian architects. Melville Street, in the West End, despite the parked cars, still retains the effect of a broad avenue. Here the wide street, which proceeds along to a crescent and the statue of Robert Dundas, second Lord Melville (1771-1851), is a perfect setting for the soaring architecture of St Mary's Episcopal Cathedral.

St Mary's Cathedral is the mother church of the Scottish Episcopalian Diocese of Edinburgh, and, after St Mungo's Cathedral at Glasgow, the second largest church in Scotland. It faces Palmerston Place and is built on the former Coates estate, bequeathed by the daughters of William Walker, Attorney in Exchequer. The sisters left about £400,000 to the Episcopal Church with the stipulation that a church should be built on this site. One condition was that it be named St Mary's, in memory of their mother; another that six architects, three English and three Scottish, should be asked to submit plans for the church. The winning architect was Sir George Gilbert Scott. The church was begun in 1874, with workmen from every corner of the British Isles taking part in the construction. It was dedicated five years later. The central spire is 263 feet high and the twin spires at the front are named after the Walker sisters—the Mary spire and the Barbara spire.

116. *St Mary's Episcopal Cathedral.*

117. *The Castle and St George's, Charlotte Square, from the Royal Botanical Garden, Inverleith.*

118. *The Scott Monument, and the Scottish Widows' Fund and Life Assurance Society's building (designed by Sir Basil Spence), in St Andrew Square.*

For some years the Edinburgh skyline has been interrupted by building cranes —symbols of growth and redevelopment. This has been particularly true in George Square and in the area of St Andrew Square, which is said to be the richest square in Scotland. At one time this was a residential area. Now, however, the tall monument to Henry Dundas, first Viscount Melville, looks down on a multitude of insurance companies, banks, the Edinburgh Stock Exchange, and the like. The Georgian façades of Craig's New Town are being replaced by the austere lines of the twentieth century, one notable example being the head office of the Scottish Widows' Fund and Life Assurance Society on the western side of St Andrew Square. Designed by Sir Basil Spence and completed in 1962, this six-storey structure has an exterior of glass, white stone and black marble which provides a modern counterpoint to the square's traditional past.

142

119. *The back of the Standard Life Assurance Company's building (designed by Sir Robert Matthew, in association with Michael Laird), George Street.*

120. *Monument to Dugald Stewart, the philosopher.*

121. *Spanned by the North Bridge, the railway marks the boundary between the Old Town and the New.*

Near the top of the stairs rising from Waterloo Place to the Calton Hill is the Grecian memorial to the philosopher Dugald Stewart (1753-1828). Built in the form of a temple, with a cupola supported by nine fluted Corinthian pillars, the memorial is particularly impressive when seen in silhouette at dusk. The centre of the memorial is occupied by a finely shaped urn.

Dugald Stewart lectured in mathematics, astronomy, and moral philosophy at Edinburgh University. He was a hard-working man. It is said that he rose each day at 3 a.m., and by nightfall had to be lifted into his carriage. He was also very tolerant, which gave offence in some quarters—especially to parents of students who thought his ideas dangerous. Stewart was a supporter of David Hume, and once, in fact, defended Hume's theory of cause and effect before the General Assembly. In 1792 Stewart published the first volume of his *Philosophy of the Human Mind*. He is buried in the Canongate Kirkyard.

Adding to the distinctively Grecian flavour of Calton Hill is the monument to Professor John Playfair, mathematician and philosopher, who died in 1819; and, perhaps most impressive, the Royal High School, which sits in a niche carved out of the hill on the southern side. The High School, which was completed in 1829, is perhaps the most classical of all of Edinburgh's Grecian structures. It was designed by Thomas Hamilton, R.S.A., a former pupil, and is modelled after the Temple of Theseus in Athens. The school itself has been in existence since the twelfth century and has produced more than its share of celebrated men. Among its former pupils are Alexander Graham Bell, Sir Walter Scott, Robert Adam, and three Lord Chancellors of Great Britain—Wedderburn, Erskine, and Brougham.

122. *The Observatory, on the Calton Hill.*

An observatory for Edinburgh was first proposed before 1736; but it failed to materialise until 1792, when the Magistrates undertook to complete a building already started on Calton Hill. This fortress-like structure had been designed by Robert Adam and was being built by the University to house a reflecting telescope capable of magnifying 1,200 times. Work had ceased, owing to lack of funds, until the Town Council accepted responsibility for completing the structure. In 1812 the Observatory was taken in hand by the newly formed Astronomical Institute of Edinburgh, and this group promoted the building of a new observatory, designed by W. H. Playfair and erected to the east of the existing one. This is the attractive cross-shaped building with the dome which dominates the Hill. The Royal Observatory on Blackford Hill was built in 1895.

146

123. *The Regent Bridge.*

124. *Edinburgh by moonlight, from the north.*

Scotland has long enjoyed a high reputation for producing good gardeners and nowhere is the outward evidence of this high skill so apparent as in the Royal Botanic Garden at Inverleith. History records botanic gardens in Edinburgh as early as 1670: but the garden at Inverleith, which covers about seventy acres, was not established until about 1820. The real stimulus of its development came about seventy years later, when Professor Isaac Bayley Balfour was appointed Regius Keeper of the Garden. Soon afterwards, the Garden came under the Ministry of Works' control. Under Professor Balfour the famous outdoor rock garden, with its many alpine specimens, was formed.

Although the garden is enjoyed by about one million people annually, it is intended primarily for scientific advancement. Through the years many expeditions have been made to obtain specimen plants for the collection. George Forres of Falkirk, who joined the staff in 1902, made seven trips to Western China. He amassed 31,000 different species of which more than 400 were new to science. Some of these were the dwarf rhododendrons now in the Rock Garden. Another collector, Archibald Menzies, while accompanying an expedition in 1795, landed in Chile and returned with the nut of the Monkey Puzzle Tree from which he grew seedlings. Some of the garden's beautiful primulas were collected in 1930 at a height of over 10,000 feet in the Burmese mountains. The plants were packed in ice and brought by refrigerated ship to Britain.

On the eastern side of the Royal Botanic Garden stands the impressive Herbarium, which was opened in 1964. The building, with its distinctive high-arched windows and white terrazzo facing, houses a collection of two million dried botanical specimens which are used in the naming and classifying of plants. The building also houses a 30,000-volume library.

One main function of the Botanic Garden is to provide ground for young gardeners and foresters whom, after three years' study, earn a diploma in horticulture. Many of the former students have helped to spread the Garden's fame beyond Britain. One such was John McLaren, 'The Grand Old Man of American horticulture', who went to California at the age of twenty-four and founded the celebrated Golden Gate Park of San Francisco. Another important activity of the Garden is contributing to a free international exchange of seed for scientific study. Approximately 14,000 packets are mailed all over the world each year.

125. *The new Herbarium, in the Royal Botanic Garden.*

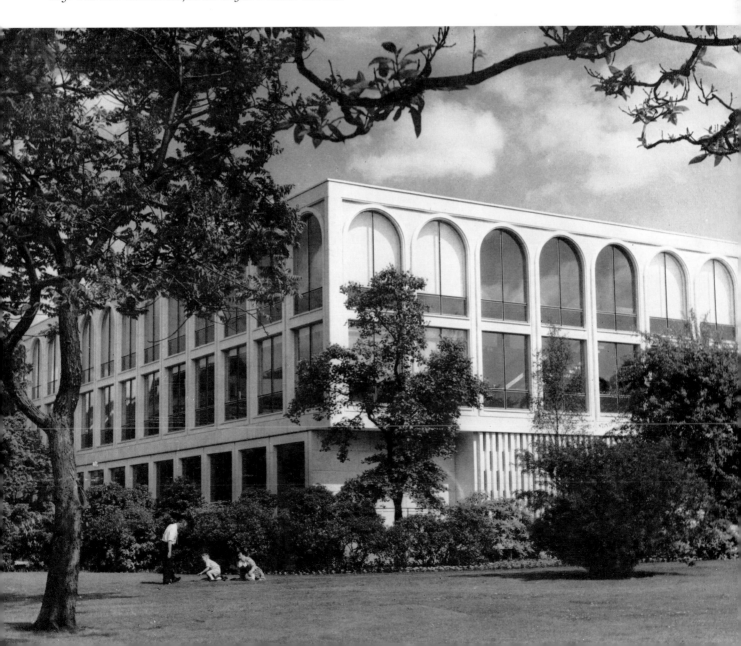

126. *Every year, on 21 October, the anniversary of the Battle of Trafalgar, the Nelson monument on the Calton Hill reminds the Scots that 'England expects every man will do his duty'.*

Over the past century and a half, the telescope-shaped monument to Lord Nelson on the Calton Hill has been likened to a lighthouse, to a butter-churn, and, by George Scott-Moncrieff in *Edinburgh*, to a pile of 'outsize cotton reels'. Whatever one's opinion of this distinctive monument, it is part of everyday Edinburgh life, if only because of its connexion with the One o'Clock Gun. Each day at 1 p.m. a gun fires from the Castle, and simultaneously a time-ball drops from the top of the monument. There is a traditional story told that a credulous visitor, hearing the gun fire and seeing the ball drop, exclaimed: 'Man, that's wonderfu' shootin'!' In fact, the time-ball allowed mariners in the Forth to check their chronometers, vital to precise navigation.

Visitors sometimes ask why an English hero should be so honoured in the Scottish capital, but it should not be overlooked that many Scots served with Nelson, and indeed on *Victory*. Perhaps that is why so few people quibble when, on the anniversary of Trafalgar, the Monument displays Nelson's famous signal: 'England expects every man will do his duty'. The Monument is now a small museum, but was originally intended to accommodate disabled seamen. Another scheme called for its use as the centre of a naval and military burial ground. Neither of these proposals ever came to fruition; but the monument (completed in 1815) was used at one time as a restaurant.

During the Middle Ages, the Calton Hill stood sentinel over a tournament ground—on the side now occupied by London Road. Revels and open-air plays were held here up to the time of Queen Mary. It is said that Bothwell first attracted the Queen's attention during one of these events, by leaping his horse into the ring and galloping up and down the slopes of the adjacent hill. In later times the hill also had a dubious reputation as the scene of witchcraft. In Richard Bovet's *Pandemonium; or, The Devil's Clouster* (1684), an account of researches on the occult is given by Captain George Burton, a visitor to Leith, who claimed to have interviewed the Fairy Boy of Leith, a ten-year-old lad who weekly beat the drums *under* the Calton Hill. 'I beat all points to a sort of people,' the boy told the Captain; and then he went on to relate a tale of Calton feasts of meat and wine, and nocturnal trips from the hill to Holland and France. At the extreme eastern end of Calton Hill were also the Quarry Holes, a favourite rendezvous for duels.

Approaching the hill from Waterloo Place, an extension of Princes Street, one passes the remnants of the Old Calton Burying-Ground. Here are interred the remains of a number of notable Scots, including Sir Walter Scott's publisher, Archibald Constable; the founder of Stewart's College, Daniel Stewart; and William Blackwood, founder of *Blackwood's Magazine*. Also buried here is David Hume. His memorial, a round tower like a small gasometer, is easily identified. Adam Smith naively described it as having been 'David's only vanity'. Near it stand Edinburgh's statue of Abraham Lincoln, erected in memory of Scots-Americans who fell in the Civil War. The monument, which was executed by George Bissett in 1893, shows the celebrated President with a freed slave at his feet. Adjacent to the burying-ground stands the impressive mass of St Andrew's House, administrative centre of the Government in Scotland. Its great bronze doors bear symbolic representations of Saints Andrew, Ninian, Columba, Magnus, and Kentigern. The buttressed towers behind St Andrew's House, best viewed from the Bridges, are the remains of the Calton Jail. This building was in use until the beginning of the twentieth century, when it was superseded by a new prison at Saughton.

127. *Leith Docks.*

VII. ELSEWHERE IN EDINBURGH

Leith has been an active port since Berwick was sacked by Edward I in 1296. It was following this event that the monks of Melrose and Newbattle began routing their wool caravans through Edinburgh to Leith for shipment to Flanders. Today, Leith's principal export is coal, but the port also handles large quantities of imported grain, timber, and raw materials for the manufacture of fertilisers; it also imports and exports motor cars. A development scheme begun in 1965 will substantially increase the port's facilities, by creating deep water berths for cruising liners up to 35,000 tons. The port is governed by Leith Dock Commission, the 15 Commissioners representing shipowners, dock ratepayers, Edinburgh and Leith Chambers of Commerce, Edinburgh Corporation and the Edinburgh Merchant Company. The Commissioners' undertaking extends from Seafield Toll Bar to Wardie Brae.

Edinburgh and Leith were amalgamated in 1920; and, while one is known for its traffic in heavy goods, the industry of the other is light. Edinburgh's principal industries fall into three main groups: food, drink, and tobacco; paper, printing, and publishing; and engineering. These industries, indeed, account for two-thirds of the city's industrial employment. Recent years have seen an increase in brewing in the city; but, apart from two or three distilleries, Edinburgh's dealing in whisky is mostly confined to bottling and blending, most of which is done in Leith. Edinburgh has long been Scotland's major printing centre, but engineering provides no less than one-fifth of all manufacturing employment in the city. Clearly engineering has a key role to play in Scotland's industrial future and some sectors of the industry in Edinburgh are expanding rapidly, notably electronics, electrical engineering, and the production of scientific instruments.

Industrial dependence is perhaps the key to the Edinburgh-Leith relationship, though Leith had a long history as a thriving and independent burgh. Anyone who follows the descending trail of Leith Walk will note the sense of individuality which the port community still retains. Leith was first established in the twelfth century on the banks of the Water of Leith, at the point where it entered the Firth of Forth. Many of the old buildings in the community remain. A famous royal visit to Leith occurred in 1561 when Mary, Queen of Scots, landed from France and rested in the home of a merchant, Andrew Lamb, before proceeding to Edinburgh. Lamb's House, with its crow-stepped gables and half-shuttered windows, is now owned by the National Trust for Scotland. It is run by the Edinburgh and Leith Old People's Welfare Council as a day centre for old people. The National Commercial Bank in Bernard Street, once the Independent Leith Bank which issued its own notes, is an outstanding example of a small, almost domestic, Regency building.

A short distance from the gates to Leith Docks, in the street known as the Shore, nonchalant swans are usually to be found in the Water of Leith, heedless of the heavy traffic a few yards away. Not far distant are Leith Links, one of the port's most attractive features. Charles I was playing golf over this stretch of open land in 1641 when he received word of the Irish Rebellion. As the story goes, the royal game continued uninterrupted. The Links have also been the scene of military action, and two knolls still to be seen are said to have been the emplacements of English artillery during an invasion 300 years ago.

153

128. *Fishwives, in their braws.*

Since the seventeenth century fishwives of the port of Newhaven, close to Leith, have been selling their husbands' harvest of the sea in Edinburgh. Their traditional working dress includes a striped petticoat, with matching navy-blue skirt looped up to show the stripes, and a shawl. The heavy creels on their backs are supported by a leather band round the forehead. On special occasions Paisley shawls and other finery are added. Only a few of these rosy-cheeked women continue to ply their trade: but their tradition lingers on, thanks chiefly to a poem by Lady Nairne which immortalised the fishwives' cry 'Wha'll buy my caller [fresh] herrin' '? Lady Nairne (1766-1845) was a celebrated song writer and poetess whose works showed great compassion for people in all walks of life. Some of her poems, published anonymously in her lifetime, were collected posthumously as *Lays from Strathearn* (1846). The best known of these are 'Land o' the Leal', 'Charlie is my Darling', and 'Caller Herrin' '. The last-named was set to music by Nathaniel Gow.

Caller Herrin'

Wha'll buy my [a]caller herrin'?	[a] *fresh*
They're bonnie fish and [b]halesome farin';	[b] *wholesome fare*
Wha'll buy my caller herrin',	
New drawn [c]fae the Forth?	[c] *from*

When ye were sleepin' on your pillows,	
Dreamed ye [a]aught o' our puir fellows,	[a] *anything*
Darkling as they faced the billows,	
A' to fill the woven willows?	

Wha'll buy my caller herrin'?	
They're no [a]brocht here without brave darin';	[a] *brought*
Buy my caller herrin',	
Haul'd through wind and rain.	

Wha'll buy my caller' herrin?	
Oh, ye may ca' them vulgar farin';	
Wives and mithers, [a]maist despairin',	[a] *almost*
Ca' them lives o' men.	

When the [a]creel o' herrin' passes,	[a] *fish-basket*
Ladies, clad in silk and laces,	
Gather in their braw pelisses,	
Cast their heads and screw their faces.	

Neebour wives, now [a]tent my tellin'	[a] *heed*
When the bonnie fish ye're sellin',	
At [b]ae word be in your dealin'—	[b] *one*
Truth will stand when [c]a'thing's failin'.	[c] *everything's*

Wha'll buy my caller herrin'?
They're bonnie fish and halesome farin'.
Wha'll buy my caller herrin',
New drawn fae the Forth?

129. *Edinburgh, from the Braids, with typical modern suburban development.*

130. *Merchiston Tower, and Napier Technical College.*

Napier Technical College, opened in 1964, is the largest technical college in south-east Scotland. Historically it could scarcely have been placed on a more appropriate site, since it was here that John Napier, the inventor of logarithms, was born in 1550. The ancient Merchiston Tower, now handsomely restored, stands symbolically at the heart of the college, a splendid union architecturally between the old and the new. The Tower contains the boardroom, offices of the Principal and Vice-Principal, and a small museum. In the boardroom is a rare timber ceiling dated 1581.

The college contains 100 workshops, 24 laboratories, and 34 classrooms, and provides courses up to the level of Scottish Certificate of Education, Higher Grade, and City and Guild certificates. More than thirty trades are catered for, with a capacity for upwards of 8,000 students.

Edinburgh has long been renowned as a centre of good schooling. Its celebrated Royal High School traces its history back to the foundation of Holyrood, and George Heriot's to the days of James VI.

The roots of education run deep throughout Scotland. The Reformers paid zealous attention to it, setting out a national system of schools and schoolmasters; and under the Union of 1707, when so much else was swept away, Scotland preserved her own national system of education. From the earliest days, its most worthy principle was that the highest education should be accessible to any child capable of benefiting from it.

Today the city's schools and colleges comprise an educational establishment of formidable variety and range. It is an establishment that is always on the move, for with the advance of educational thought and practice, new facilities and new approaches are constantly required at each school—whether primary, secondary, further education, or adult classes. The majority of the schools within the city's bounds are managed by Edinburgh Corporation, which is the education authority. There are also a considerable number of independent and grant-aided schools which attract pupils from all over Britain and abroad as well as from the city area. In the nineteenth century three public schools on the English model were established; and there are also several schools administered by the Edinburgh Merchant Company.

131. *The Pentlands, from Firrhill Secondary School.*

Golf, an infinitely exacting game which has created more philosophers than athletes, was Scotland's sporting gift to the world. A democratic game which in Scotland has always reflected the egalitarian attitudes of the Scot, golf began on public links, kings and commoners swinging with equal enthusiasm and privilege. James VII (1633-1701), when he lived in Edinburgh as Duke of York and heir presumptive to the throne of the United Kingdom, played golf over Leith Links—as did the citizens of Leith and Edinburgh. The Old Course at St Andrews is the most famous in the world, yet until a few years after the Second World War the ratepayers of St Andrews could still play over it free of charge.

There is now little, if any, absolutely free golf in Scotland, but all major towns and many minor ones have municipal courses on which citizens can play at very reasonable charges. In Edinburgh, where golf has been played since 1457 at least, there are six municipal courses and 28 putting greens and short-hole courses, as well as 16 private courses. Among the most popular of the municipal courses are those on the Braid Hills, which offer a lofty and inspiring view of the city, the Firth of Forth, and Fife.

Edinburgh abounds in sports, whether for the participant or spectator. Association and Rugby football facilities, under the management of clubs, schools and the University, are plentiful. The Scottish Rugby Union stadium at Murrayfield, where the internationals are played, is known through radio and television to countless enthusiasts who have never set foot in Scotland. The city has two First Division football teams—the Heart of Midlothian, affectionately known as the Hearts, play at Tynecastle Park, while Hibernian, or the Hibs, have their home at Easter Road Park. Both are equipped to play games at night under floodlight.

Some of the pleasantest green spaces dotted about the city, from Princes Street Gardens to the suburbs, are devoted to bowling greens. The Corporation supports a total of 51 of these greens but there are many more under the ownership of private clubs. One of the best tennis grounds in Britain is located at Craiglockhart, offering six grass courts and ten hard courts. The Corporation also maintains 22 other courts in various parts of the city. Even croquet enthusiasts have a club, which rents three spacious lawns from the Corporation in the grounds of Lauriston Castle.

One cannot overlook the contemplative sport of angling, which flourishes even in the heart of the capital city. Edinburgh is surrounded by half-a-dozen reservoirs, most of which have boats on them. The trout-fishing in these part-natural, part-artificial lochs is let by the Corporation at reasonable prices. Even more surprising to the visitor is the fact that there are brown trout, some of reasonable size, in the Water of Leith, not only in its upper reaches but in the midst of the city. It is quite an experience for a trout angler to lean over the bridge at Canonmills with the buses thundering at his back and see trout in the modest stream below. It must be an even more uncommon experience to cast a line in full view of so many spectators and passers-by.

Edinburgh's position permits easy access to beaches nearby, especially at Gullane and North Berwick, and along the Fife coast. The city's seaside suburb, Portobello, has a large open-air bathing pool which can accommodate 3,000 swimmers; the chief attraction here is the heated water and a wave-making machine which gives the effect of open sea. Another pool, built to Olympic standards, is being constructed at Park Road, on the edge of Holyrood Park.

132. *The Royal Observatory, Salisbury Crags, Arthur's Seat, and Newington, from the Braids.*

At the picturesque little village of Cramond, there has been in recent years a tremendous upsurge of interest in sailing. The mouth of the River Almond is frequently almost crowded with craft, and the wide estuary of the Forth offers lively sport. Inland, the long range of the Pentland Hills to the south of the city offer, in their varying seasons, recreation to the hiker, the pony trekker, and the skier. Of these three sportsmen, the hiker was the first to become familiar with these rolling hills. They are crossed by many heather paths which, in recent years, have also become useful routes in the developing sport of pony-trekking. Devotees of skiing appear on the Pentland slopes in ever-increasing numbers; now their enjoyment need no longer be confined to the winter months, following the provision of an artificial ski-slope at Hillend. A chairlift, constructed primarily for skiers, is also opening up the high Pentlands ridge to many more walkers.

133. *Sunday morning, on George IV Bridge.*

134. '... *so that's the sort of people they were.*'

Many authors, wishing to write a definitive as well as a descriptive work on Edinburgh, have sought to explain its people. Lord Cockburn, for example, devoted several pages of his *Memorials* to praise old ladies whom he described as 'strong-headed, warm hearted, and high spirited, ... merry even in solitude; very resolute', and 'indifferent about the modes and habits of the modern world'. In *The Perambulator in Edinburgh* (1926) James Bone said 'if one might use "plinth" for skirts and footgear, one would say that the neatness of plinth of the Edinburgh women has struck many observers as a feature of these streets'. Robert Louis Stevenson (*Edinburgh Picturesque Notes*) described the city as being 'inhabited by citizens of the familiar type, who keep ledgers, and attend church, and have sold their immortal portion to a daily paper'. An English visitor, Captain Topham (*Letters from Edinburgh* 1776) spoke highly of 'the civilities that have been paid to my fellow-traveller and me', and also observed of the populace, 'I know of no quality more conspicuous in the inhabitants of this country, than Complaisance; which is common to every age and sex, but more particularly to the women, who seem to emulate each other in good-breeding'. Perhaps William Cobbett gave the best summation in *Tour of Scotland* (1832) when he said of Edinburgh, 'The *people*, however, still exceed the place'.

135. *The Forth Bridges, shortly before the Road Bridge was finally completed.*

The opening of the road bridge across the Forth estuary in 1964 realised a dream that originated more than 200 years before. One of the longest suspension bridges in the world, it is a slim, elegant structure more than a mile and a half in length, including the viaducts, and has a central span of 3,300 feet between two main towers. It stands a short distance upriver from the massive, cantilevered railway bridge which opened in 1890, and provides an additional link between the capital city and the north. The newer bridge and its eight miles of approach roads took six years to construct, and the winds that are encountered in the Forth estuary made the project an outstanding engineering feat. A total of 39,000 tons of steel and 150,000 cubic yards of concrete went into the bridge. It carries two roadways, each 24 feet wide, as well as cycle tracks and footpaths.

OUR NOBIL TOUN

AN EDINBURGH ANTHOLOGY

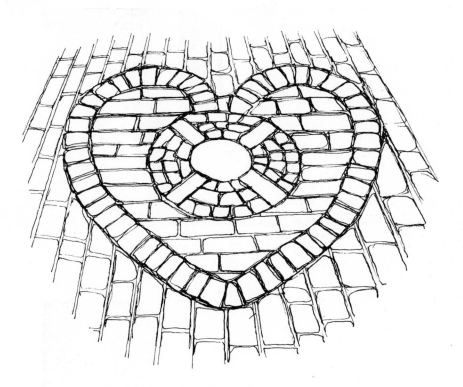

The Heart of Midlothian, in the Royal Mile.

1. The Taking of the Castle
14 March 1314

In 1376, when John Barbour compiled his Brus, *a long heroic poem which stands at the beginning of Scottish literature, the rock on which Edinburgh Castle is built had already been fortified for about a thousand years: and, presumably because the castle had never been taken, it was traditionally called Castra Puellarum, the Maidens' Castle. With the exception of St Margaret's Chapel, very little of the medieval stonework has survived nearly six more centuries of siege, rebuilding, and alteration: but the Castle, as we see it today, corroborates Barbour's vividly realistic account of the brilliantly successful stratagem by which Randolph, Earl of Moray, took it from the English only a few months before the Battle of Bannockburn.*

Randolph, Earl of Moray, was besieging Edinburgh Castle, one of the few Scottish castles still in English hands. Having been informed that James Douglas, by means of a ruse, had taken Roxburgh Castle, he offered a reward to any of his men who could suggest some stratagem by which he could capture the wall of Edinburgh Castle. One of them, called William Francis, came to him and said:

> . . . I undirtak, for my service,
> To ^aken you to clym the wall
> (And I sall formast be of all),
> ^bQuhar with a schort ^cleddir may we—
> I ^dtrow of twelf fute it may be—
> Clym to the wall up all ^equytly.
> And ^fgif that ye will ^gwit how I
> ^hWat this, I sall you ⁱlichtly say.
> ^jQuhen I wes young, this ^khendir day,
> My ^lfader wes kepar of yon hous,
> And I wes ^msumdeil ⁿvolageous,
> And lufit ane wench here in the toun;
> And ^ofor I, ^pbut suspicion,
> Micht repair ^qtill hir prevely,
> Of ^rrapis ane leddir to me made I,
> And tharwith ^sowr the wall I ^tslaid.
> Ane ^ustrat road, that I spyit had
> ^vIntill the crag, ^wsyne doun I went,
> And ^xoftsyis com to mine intent;
> And quhen it neir drew to the day,
> I held again that ^yilke way,
> And ^zay com in ^abut persaving.
> I ^boysit lang that travalling,
> So that I can that road ga richt,
> Thouch men see nevir so mirk the nicht. . . .
> 'Up to the wall I sall you bring,
> Gif God us kepis fra persaving
> Of thame that watchis on the wall.
> And gif that us so fair may fall
> That we our leddir up may set,
> Gif a man on the wall may get,
> He sall defend, gif it ^cbeis need,
> ^dQuhill the ^eremainand up thame speed.'
>
> The Erll wes blyth of his ^fcarping,
> And ^ghicht him full fair rewarding;
> And undirtuk that ^hgat to ga
> And bade him ⁱsoyn his leddir ^jma. . . .

^a teach
^b where   ^c ladder
^d believe
^e quietly
^f if   ^g know
^h know   ⁱ quickly
^j when   ^k bygone
^l father
^m somewhat   ⁿ flighty

^o so that   ^p without
^q to
^r ropes
^s over   ^t slid
^u strait
^v in   ^w then
^x oft-times

^y same
^z always   ^a without [anyone]
^b used long   perceiving

^c be
^d until   ^e rest
^f speaking
^g promised
^h way
ⁱ soon   ^j make

166

The ladder was soon made; and one dark night the Earl set out with thirty men, to climb the Castle Rock.

The nicht wes mirk, as I heard say,
And till the fute ªsoyn ᵇcummin are thay   *ª soon   ᵇ come*
Of the crag, that wes hie and ᵉschore.   *ᶜ precipitous*
ᵈThan William Francis thame before   *ᵈ then*
Clam in the ᵉcrykis ᶠforouth thame ᵍay,   *ᵉ crannies ᶠ before ᵍ always*
And at the back him followit thay. . . .

Half-way up, they found a ledge just wide enough for them to sit down on, and halted to draw breath.

And richt as thay ªwar sittand ᵇswa,   *ª were   ᵇ so*
ᶜAbovyn thame, upon the wall,   *ᶜ above*
The ᵈchack-watchis assemblit all.   *ᵈ check-watches, 'visiting rounds'*
Now help thame God that all thing may,
For in full gret perell are they!
For, micht thay see thame, thair suld ᵉnane   *ᵉ none*
ᶠEschap out of that place unslain,   *ᶠ escape*
ᵍTill ded with ʰstanis thay suld thame ⁱding: *ᵍ to death ʰ stones ⁱ batter*
Bot wondir mirk wes all the nicht
ʲSwa that they had of thame ᵏna sicht.   *ʲ so   ᵏ no*
And, ˡnocht-for-thy, yet wes thar ane   *ˡ nevertheless*
Of thame that ᵐswappit doun a stane   *ᵐ threw*
And said 'Away, I see you weill!'—
ⁿThe-quhethir he saw thame nocht ᵒa deil.   *ⁿ although ᵒ at all*
ᵖOut-owr thair ᑫheidis ʳflaw the stane.   *ᵖ out-over ᑫ heads ʳ flew*
The watchis, quhen thay heard nocht ˢstere,   *ˢ stir*
Fra that ward passit all ᵗsammin were,   *ᵗ together*
And ᵘcarpand held fer by thair way.   *ᵘ conversing*
    Erll Thomas ᵛthan ʷalsoyn, and thay   *ᵛ then   ʷ at once*
That on the crag thar sat him by,
Toward the wall clam hastily,
And thiddir com with ˣmekill main,   *ˣ much strength*
And nocht but gret perell and pain. . . .
But ʸquhatkyn pain ᶻat evir thay had,   *ʸ what kind [of] ᶻ that*
Richt to the wall thay com, ªbut bade,   *ª without delay*
That had weill neir twelf fute on ᵇhicht;   *ᵇ height*
And, for-out persaving or sicht,
Thay set thair ᶜleddir to the wall.   *ᶜ ladder*
And ᵈsyne Francis, before thame all,   *ᵈ then*
Clam up, and syne Schir Andro Gray,
And syne the Erll himself, perfay,
Wes the ᵉthrid man the wall ᶠcan ta. . . .   *ᵉ third ᶠ [who] did take*

But before the Earl's men had all come up, the guard heard movements, voices, and the clank of weapons, and swiftly and fiercely assailed them.

And thay met thame richt hardily,
And ªslaw of thame dispitwisly.   *ª slew*
Than throu the castell ᵇrase the cry,   *ᵇ rose*
'Tresoun! Tresoun!' thay cryit fast.
Than sum of thame ᶜwar sa agast   *ᶜ were*
That thay fled and ᵈlap owr the wall.   *ᵈ lept over*
Bot, to say suth, thay fled nocht all;

For the Constable, that wes hardy,
All armit schot furth to the cry,
And with him ℯfeill, hardy and stout.   ℯ *many*

    Meanwhile the Earl was still fighting the men on the wall: but before long he had
beaten them; and, as soon as all his men had got up on top of the wall, he led them down
into the Castle.

The Constable and his company
Met him and his richt hardily.
Thar men micht see gret ᵃbargane rise,   ᵃ *conflict*
For with ᵇwapnis, on ᶜmony wise,   ᵇ *weapons*   ᶜ *many*
Thay ᵈdang on othir at thair micht,   ᵈ *battered one another*
ℯQuhill ᶠswerdis, that ᵍwar fair and bricht,   ℯ *until*   ᶠ *swords*   ᵍ *were*
War till the hiltis all bludy.
Then hidwisly ʰbegowth the cry,   ʰ *began*
For thay that fellit or ⁱstekit war   ⁱ *pierced*
With gret noyis ʲcan cry and rar.   ʲ *did . . . roar*
The gude Erll and his company
ᵏFaucht in that ficht so sturdily   ᵏ *fought*
That all thair ˡfaeis ruschit war.   ˡ *foes*
The Constable was slain richt thar;
And, ᵐfra he fell, the remainand   ᵐ *from* [*the moment that*]
Fled ⁿquhar thay best micht to ᵒwarrand;   ⁿ *where*   ᵒ *refuge*
Thay durst nocht bide ᵖna mak debat.   ᵖ *nor*
The Erll wes handlit thair qsa hat   q *so hot*
That, had it nocht hapnit ʳthrou cas,   ʳ *by chance*
That the Constable thair slain was,
He had been in gret perell thar:
Bot than thay fled, thar was no ˢmar,   ˢ lit. *more*
ᵗIlke man for to ᵘsauf his life   ᵗ *every*   ᵘ *save*
And furth his dayis for to ᵛdrife,   ᵛ lit. *drive*
And sum slaid doun out-owr the wall—
The Erll has ʷtane the Castle all! . . .   ʷ *taken*
    I heard nevir in na time ˣgane   ˣ *gone*
Quhar castell wes sa stoutly tane.

BARBOUR

2.   Vinum Edinburgi

c. 1500

*In this parody of a penitential psalm, William Dunbar, cleric and courtier, prays God and
St Giles to bring King James IV back from the purgatorial miseries of Stirling to the heavenly
joys of Edinburgh.*

The Fader, the Son, and Haly Gaist,
The mirthful Mary, virgin chaist,
Of angellis all the ordouris nine,
And all the hevinly court divine,
ᵃSone bring you fra the ᵇpyne and woe   ᵃ *soon*   ᵇ *pain*
Of Strivilling, every ᶜcourt-manis foe,   ᶜ *courtier's*
Again to Edinburghis joy and bliss,

168

^dQuhair ^ewirschep, wealth, and weilfare is,
Play, plesance, and ^feik honesty:
Say ye 'Amen' for cherity. . . .

<table>
<tr><td>^d where</td><td>^e honour</td></tr>
<tr><td>^f also</td><td></td></tr>
</table>

God and ^aSanct Geill
^bHeir you convoy
^cBaith sone and weill
God and Sanct Geill
To ^dsonce and ^eseill
Solace and joy
God and Sanct Geill
Heir you convoy. . . .

^a St Giles
^b here
^c both

^d plenty   ^e happiness

. . . A porta tristitie de Strivilling
Erue, Domine, animas et corpora eorum.
Credo gustare statim vinum Edinburgi
In villa viventium,
Requiescant Edinburgi.   Amen.

Deus qui iustos et corde humiles
Ex omni eorum tribulatione liberare dignatus es,
Libera famulos tuos apud villam de Stirling versantes
A penis et tristitiis eiusdem,
Et ad Edinburgi gaudia eos perducas—
Ut requiescat Strivilling.   Amen.

DUNBAR

3.

Flodden
5-10 September 1513

The battle was fought on 9 September. These two extracts record the Town Council, in the name of the King, conscripting the citizens, and, after the first rumours of defeat, preparing for almost certain invasion, which in fact never came.

5 September 1513

We charge straitlie and commandis in our Soverane Lord the Kingis name that all maner of personis that ar cummying fra his army that thai ^aaddress thame and returne agane thairto, and that all ^bnychtbouris of this toun, ^cfensabill personis, that thai ^dsiclyke pass in thair best aray ^ebodin for weir till our said Soverane Lordis army, and present thame to the provest of this toun, under the ^fpanys contenit in our Soverane Lordis lettres ^gdirect upoun the foirganging of his army, viz. ^htynsal of lyfe, land and guid, certifeand that the names of all ⁱsic fensabill personis ^jhabill for weir remanend at hame fra the said army salbe put in writt that thai may be responsabill at our Soverane Lordis returning ^kbe Goddis grace hame agane.

^a direct themselves
^b inhabitants   ^c fit for military
^d likewise   service
^e equipped for war

^f penalties
^g immediately after his army went
^h loss   forward
ⁱ such   ^j able

^k by

We do yow to witt, [a]forsamekill as thair is ane greit rumour now laitlie rysin within this toun [b]tuiching our Soverane Lord and his army, of the [c]quhilk we understand thair is [d]cumin na veritie as yit, thairfore we charge straitlie and commandis in our said Soverane Lord the Kingis name, [e]and the presidentis for the provest and baillies within this burgh, that all maner of personis nychtbouris within the [f]samyn have reddye thair [g]fensabill geir and wapponis for weir, and [h]compeir thairwith to the said presidentis at [i]jowyng of the commoun bell, for the keiping and defens of the toun aganis thame that [j]wald invaid the samyn.

And [k]als chairgis that all wemen, and specialie vagaboundis, that thai pass to thair labouris and be nocht sene upoun the [l]gait clamorand and cryand, under the [m]pane of banesing of the personis [n]but favouris, and that the uther wemen of gude pass to the kirk and pray [o]quhane tyme requiris for our Soverane Lord and his armye and nychtbouris being thairat, and [p]hald thame at thair previe labouris [q]of the gait within thair houssis [r]as efferis.

RECORDS OF THE BURGH OF EDINBURGH

[a] *forasmuch*

[b] *touching*

[c] *which*   [d] *come*

[e] *and [in those of]*

[f] *same*   [g] *military equipment*
[h] *present themselves*
[i] *tolling*

[j] *would*
[k] *also [we] charge*

[l] *public thoroughfare*
[m] *pain of banishment*
[n] *without*
[o] *when*

[p] *hold*
[q] *off*   [r] *as may be fitting*

4.   Queen Mary's First Day in Edinburgh
19 August 1561

Scottish accounts of Queen Mary's arrival in Edinburgh make much of the expensive pageantry laid on by the authorities: theatrical settings, fancy-dress parades, Latin orations, poetry and music. But if, as is probable, we may believe this Frenchman, the Queen did not think much of the whole affair. We know that she had a good ear for music, and cannot be quite sure that the psalmody was not a weapon of offence.

We were coming in to land at Leith, when all the principal people of Leith and of Edinburgh suddenly rushed up to welcome their Queen; and, after having spent only two hours at Leith, we had to set out for Edinburgh. . . . The Queen went there on horseback; her ladies and gentlemen were mounted on local hired geldings, themselves not much good, and no better harnessed. Indeed, on seeing such preparations, the Queen burst into tears and said, these were not the pomp and pageantry, the magnificence, the mounts she had enjoyed so long, but since her paradise must be changed into hell, she must be patient. Worse was to follow. For she was lodged down in the Holyrood Abbey (which is assuredly a beautiful building, and not at all typical of the country), and, just when she meant to go to bed, there came beneath her window five or six hundred rascals from the town, to serenade her on vile fiddles and rebecks (of which that country has no lack); and they began singing psalms, all as badly sung and as tuneless as could be. Alas! what music! What repose for her night!

BRANTÔME

The First Missile of the Civil War
1637

Nobody knows the truth about Jenny Geddes and her stool, but whoever threw that stool at the Dean of Edinburgh in the Cathedral of St Giles let fly the first missile of the Civil War. The stool, or one very like it, may be seen in the Museum of Antiquities. In his Analecta, Wodrow tells of a tradition that it was thrown by Mrs Mean, wife of an Edinburgh merchant, but anyone in Edinburgh is pretty sure to tell you it was Jenny Geddes.

St Giles Kirk had just been made a cathedral for this short part of its history, and its Bishop and Dean were trying to conduct a service according to Laud's Liturgy, which to the Scots was not distinguishable from the Roman Catholic servicebook.

In the Old Church there was great malecontentment and a wonderfull sturre: many mouthes were there opened to the Bischops disgrace. 'False antichristian', 'wolfe,' 'beistile bellie god', and 'craftie fox', were the best epithets and titles of dignitie which were given him. The Dean, Mr. James Hanna, was mightilie upbraided. Some cried, 'Hee is a sonne of a witches breeding and the divels gett. No healtsome water can come foorth from such a polluted fountaine.' Others cryed, 'Ill-hanged theefe! if at that time when thou wentest to court thou hadest beene well hanged, thou hadest not beene here to be a pest to Gods church this day.' One did cast a stoole at him, intending to have given him a ticket of remembrance; but jouking [*ducking*] became his safegaird at that time. The Church was immediatelie emptied of the most parte of the congregatione, and the dores thereof barred at commandement of the secular power. A good Christian woman, much desirous to remove, perceaving she could get no passage patent, betooke herselfe to her Bible in a remote corner of the church. As she was there stopping her eares at the voice of popische charmers, whome she remarked to be verie headstrong in the publict practice of their antichristiane rudiments, a young man sitting behind her beganne to sound foorth 'Amen!' At the hearing thereof, she quicklie turned her about, and after she had warmed both his cheekes with the weight of her hands, she thus schott against him the thunderbolt of her zeal:— 'False theefe! (said she) is there no uther parte of the Kirke to sing Masse in, but thou must sing it at my lugge?' . . .

ROTHES

6.   Montrose and Argyle
18 May 1650

Here is the source of the most vividly-coloured picture of the treatment of Montrose after his arrival captive in Edinburgh. The unknown author, evidently, it would seem, an eye-witness, is on his side, and this account is a corrective to later partisan descriptions.

Montrose had intervened on behalf of Charles I just when he had evidently lost the Civil War at Marston Moor, beaten by Leslie's Scottish army as much as by Cromwell's Ironsides. In a miraculous campaign in the north of Scotland, Montrose and his Highlanders had brought discomfiture upon Argyle, and misery to a great many common people, only to be defeated as soon as Leslie was free to bring his army back to Scotland. In 1650 he rallied to the cause of Charles II, but was ambushed, routed, and taken prisoner.

Looking at the balcony of Moray House in the Canongate, it is easy for us to believe the tradition that this is the place mentioned in our extract.

Upon the 18th day, about 4 [in] the afternoone, he was broght in at the watter [a]yet, whair he was met   [a] *gate* by the magistraitis the gardis and the hangman, the rest of the prisoneris being tyed two by two, going [b]barheiddit befor him. How soone he cam within   [b] *bareheaded* the ^cport, the Magistratis show him thair order. When he had red it he perceived the cart and the hangman. He said he wold go willinglye to it; he was onlye sorrye that throw him his master, whose commissione he carried, sould be dishonored. Then going cheirfullye on the cart, he, being oncovered, was by the hangman tyed therto by ropis, and the hangman ^drod covered upon the horse that drew the cairt: thus was he led to prisone. In all the way ther appeired in him such majestie, courrag, modistie, and even somewhat more than naturall, that thes common women, who had lost ther husbandis and children in his ^ewaris, and who were hyred to stone him, were upon the sight of him so astonished and moved, that thair intendit curse turnd into teares and prayeris, so as the nixt day all the ministeris preiched agaynst thame for not stoning and revyling him. It is remarkable that, of the many thowsand beholderis, onlye the Laddie Jean Gordon, Countess of Hadinton, did publicklie insult and laucht at him; which being perceaved by a gentill-man in the streit, he cryed up to hir that it becam hir better to sit upon the cart for her adulltiries. The Lord Lorne and his new Laddie wer also siting in a balconie, joyfull spectatoris; and the cairt being stopit when it cam befor the ludging wher the Chancelour, Argyle, and Warriston sat, that they might have tyme to insult, he suspecting the bussines turned his face towards them, wherupon they presentlye creipet in at the windowes; which being perceaved by ane Inglishman, he cryed up, it was no wonder they start asyd at his look, for they durst not look him in the face ^fthir seavin yeiris bygan.

After he was ^glousit from the cart, he gave the hangman gold, saying, Fellow ther is drink monie for dryving the cairt. It was past seavine a'clock at nyght befor he was entered into the ^htowbuith, and immeaditlye the Parliment met, and ⁱsend som of ther owine number, and som ministeris to examine him, bot he refused to answer anye thing to them, untill he sould know in what termis they stood with the King; which being reportit to the Parliment, they continued proceiding agaynst him till Munday, and allowed ther commissioneris to tell him that the King and they wer agried. He desyred that nycht till be at rest, for he was wearied with a longsom jorney, and he said the compliment they had put upon him that day was som thing tydeus.

WIGTON

^c *[city] gate*

^d *rode*

^e *wars*

^f *these seven years bygone*
^g *released*

^h *Tolbooth (town prison)*
ⁱ *sent*

136. 'View of EDINBURGH from the West; Water of Leith in
foreground.' *Watercolour, 12·5 × 19·5 cm., by J. M. W. Turner,
1801. Sketchbook, Inventory No. LV-1, British Museum.*

137. 'The Parliament Close & Public Characters'. *Chromo-lithograph 43·5 × 60·0 cm., engraved by John le Conte, and etched by John Dobbie, 1864. New Club, Edinburgh. This representation of the Parliament Close as it may have*

appeared c. 1785 is based on an original oil-painting (now in Huntly House), in which David Roberts, John Wilson, and others painted the buildings, and Sir David Wilkie, Alexander Frazer, and John Kay added the figures.

138. 'Manor Place, Edinburgh'. *Watercolour, 18·1 × 24·2 cm., by an
anonymous artist, 1848. Central Public Library, Edinburgh.*

The Union
22-3 October 1706

With the passage of the Scottish and English Acts of Union, Edinburgh ceased, on 1 May 1707, to be the capital of a politically independent country. Commercial gain was promised, and an end to the disadvantage of having a powerful and jealous neighbour. There were Scots, however, who were willing to remain proud and poor. These saw themselves as betrayed by their own Parliament and, being unable to influence proceedings within, showed their natural feelings outside its closed doors.

To Daniel Defoe, sent from London as one of the negotiators, these men, no doubt, would seem 'ripe for mischief'. Every angry mob is ugly. Defoe himself was in some physical danger, from the natives; and this adds to the immediacy of his first-rate reporting.

He is wrong, in an interesting way, about the 'Land-Market'. It should be the Lawn-Market. A familiar old print shows the street with bales of linen set out on stalls. Defoe is over-compensating for the Scots accent.

The common People now screw'd up to a Pitch, and Ripe for the Mischief designed, and prompted by the particular Agents of a wicked Party, began to be very insolent: It had been whispered about several Days, that the Rabble would rise, and come up to the Parliament House, and cry out, *No Union*; That they would take away the Honours, *as they call them, viz.* The Crown, etc. and carry them to the Castle, and a long Variety of Foolish Reports of this kind.

But the first Appearance of anything Mobish was, that every day, when the Duke [of *Hamilton*] went up, but principally as he came down in his Chair from the House, the Mob follow'd him, shouting and crying out, GOD bless his Grace, for standing up against the Union, and appearing for his Country, and the like. . . .

On the 22*d* of *October*, they follow'd the Dukes Chair quite thro' the City down to the Abbey Gate; The Guards prevented their going further; But all the way as they came back, they were heard to threaten what they would do the next day; That then they would be a thousand times as many; That they would pull the Traitors, *so they call'd the Treaters of the Union at* London, out of their Houses, and they would soon put an end to the Union.

On the 23*d*, they made part of their Words good indeed; For, as the Parliament sat something late, the People gather'd in the Streets, and about the Doors of the Parliament House, and particularly the Parliament Closs was almost full, that the Members could not go in or out without Difficulty; when Duke *Hamilton* coming out of the House, the Mob Huzza'd as formerly, and follow'd his Chair in a very great Number; The Duke instead of going down to *the Abbey* as usual, went up the High-Street to the *Land-Market*, as they call it, and so to the Lodgings of the Duke of *Athole*; Some said, he went to avoid the Mob; Others maliciously said, he went to point them to their Work.

While he went in to the Duke of *Athole*'s Lodgings, the Rabble attended at the Door; and, by Shouting and Noise, having increased their Numbers to several thousands, they began with Sir *Patrick Johnston*, who was one of the Treaters, and the Year before had been Lord Provost; First they assaulted his Lodgings with Stones and Sticks, *and Curses not a few*; but his Windows being too high, they came up the Stairs to his Door, and fell to Work at it with Sledges, or great Hammers; And, had they broke it open in their first Fury, he had, without doubt, been Torn in Pieces without Mercy; and this only because he was a Treater in the Commission to *England*; For, before that, no Man was so well Belov'd, as he, over the whole City.

His Lady, in the utmost Despair with this Fright, comes to the Window, with two Candles in her Hand, that she might be known; and cryed out, *for GODs Sake*, to call the Guards: An Honest Apothecary in the Town, who knew her Voice, and saw the Distress she was in, and to whom the Family, under GOD, is obliged, for their Deliverance, ran immediately down to the Town Guard; but they would not stir, without the Lord Provosts Order;—but that being soon obtain'd, one Captain *Richardson*, who Commanded, taking about thirty Men with him, March'd bravely up to them; and making his way with great Resolution thro' the Croud, they Flying, but Throwing Stones, and Hallowing at him, and his Men, he seized the Foot of the Stair Case; and then boldly went up, clear'd the Stair, and took six of the Rabble in the very Act; and so delivered the Gentleman and his Family.—

But this did not put a Stop to the general Tumult, tho it delivered this particular Family: For the Rabble, by this time, were prodigiously increased, and went Roving up and down the Town, Breaking the Windows of the Members of Parliament, and Insulting them in their Coaches, in the Streets; They put out all the Lights, that they might not be discovered; and the Author of this had one great Stone thrown at him, for but looking out of a Window; for they suffered no Body to look out, especially with any Lights, lest they should know Faces, and Inform against them afterwards.

By this time, it was about eight or nine a Clock at Night, and now they were absolute Masters of the City; and it was Reported, they were going to shut up all the Ports;—The Lord Commissioner being Inform'd of that, sent a Party of the Foot Guards, and took Possession of the *Nether-Bow*, which is a Gate in the Middle of the High-Street, as *Temple-Bar* between the City of *London* and the Court.

The City was now in a Terrible Fright, and every Body was under Concern for their Friends; The Rabble went Raving about the Streets till Midnight, frequently Beating Drums, and raising more People; when my Lord Commissioner being inform'd, there were a Thousand of the Seamen and Rabble come up from *Leith*; and Apprehending, if it were suffered to go on, it might come to a Dangerous Head, and be out of his Power to suppress,—he sent for the Lord Provost, and Demanded, that the Guards should March into the City.

The Lord Provost, after some Difficulty, yielded; tho it was alledged that it was what was never known in *Edinburgh* before.—About one a Clock in the Morning, a Battallion of the Guards entred the Town, Marched up to the Parliament Closs, and took Post in all the Avenues of the City, which prevented the Resolutions taken to Insult the Houses of the rest of the Treaters.

The Rabble were intirely reduc'd by this, and gradually dispers'd, and so the Tumult ended. . . .

The Author of this had his Share of the Danger in this Tumult, and tho unknown to him, was watch'd and set by the Mob, in order to know where to find him, had his Chamber Windows Insulted, and the Windows below him broken by Mistake.—But, by the Prudence of his Friends, the Shortness of its Continuance, and GODs Providence, he escaped.

DEFOE

8.   The Most Insolent and Illegal Practice
                              31 August 1737

How hard it is to be just if you have to control a mischievous crowd! What is an Officer of the Law to do if he does not know exactly who flung the dung?

The Lord Provost Baillies and Council with the Deacons of Crafts Ordinary and Extraordinary, taking to their Consideration that the peace and good Government of this City has been frequently disturbed and Insulted, and many pernicious and fatal consequences have ensued to the Citizens and Inhabitants thereof, by the most insolent and Illegal Practise of throwing stones, mud and other Garbage, at the proper officers of the Law, City Guard, and common executioner, when in the Exercise of their Duty and office at Lawful and publick Executions of Criminalls . . . : Therefore in order to prevent all such pernicious and illegal practices in time comeing, and for the more effectual bringing to Justice the person or persons guilty of all or any of the aforesaid Crimes, DID, and hereby DO ENACT, STATUTE and ORDAIN, that the person or persons who shall hereafter be found guilty . . . of throwing Stones, Mud, Dung, or other Garbage, at the officers of the Law, City Guard, or common executioner or others Lawfully Convocated at Such publick and Lawful execution of Sentences upon Criminals or offenders against the Laws . . . shall, upon their being Convicted thereof, be whipt through the City by the hand of the common hangman, and thereafter Imprisoned for the space of one year: and for the better discovering and bringing to Justice such offenders, the Treasurer for the time being, is hereby-appointed to pay to any person or persons, who shall discover, or cause be Discovered, any such offenders, so as they shall be Convicted of all or any of the aforesaid Crimes, the Sum of five pounds Sterling: and that none may pretend Ignorance hereof, DID ORDAIN thir [these] presents to be printed and published by Tuck of Drum through this City and its Liberties, and through Canongate, South and North Leiths, and that Copies be affixed on the publick Places in the usual Manner.

COUNCIL RECORD

9. Prince Charles Arrives in Edinburgh
15-16 September 1745

The Edinburgh citizens were mostly anti-Jacobite, but were in no position to keep the High-landers out. The city-wall had been built in haste after the defeat of Flodden, and was not very strong. In a pamphlet (1747) written in defence of Lord Provost Stewart, gaoled and charged with 'misbehaviour' in surrendering the city, David Hume describes 'a plain Wall about twenty Foot high, where highest, and about two and a half or three Foot thick, where thickest', and adds, 'It has not Strength or Thickness enough to bear Cannon.' This is a fair description of the stretch of wall which we can see for ourselves in the Vennel. John Cope had not yet arrived with his Government troops, and the Provost's Town Guards and Volunteers cannot be blamed if they were not keen to face the charge of the Highlanders.

This account is by the Rev. John Home, one of the Volunteers, who later achieved fame as the author of the tragedy of Douglas. He had some military adventures in this campaign, being captured at Falkirk, imprisoned in Doune Castle, and escaping by the classic method of tying blankets together.

The Netherbow Port was the gate of the city-wall where it crossed the High Street at the head of the Canongate.

About two o'clock in the morning the deputies set out for Gray's Mill; when they arrived there they prevailed upon Lord George Murray to second their application for a delay; but Charles refused to grant it; and the deputies were ordered in his name to get them gone.

The coach brought them back to Edinburgh, set them down in the High-Street, and then drove towards the Canongate. When the Nether-Bow Port was opened to let out the coach, 800 Highlanders, led by Cameron of Lochiel, rushed in and took possession of the city.

It was about five o'clock in the morning when the rebels entered Edinburgh. They immediately sent parties to all other gates, . . . who making the soldiers upon duty prisoners, occupied their posts as quietly as one guard relieves another. When the inhabitants of Edinburgh awaked in the morning, they found that the Highlanders were masters of the city . . . .

About ten o'clock the main body of the rebels marching by Duddingston (to avoid being fired on by the Castle) entered the King's Park, and halted in the hollow of the hills, under the peak called Arthur's Seat. By and by Charles came down to the Duke's walk, accompanied by the Highland Chiefs, and other commanders of his army.

The Park was full of people, (amongst whom was the Author of this History,) all of them impatient to see this extraordinary person. The figure and presence of Charles Stuwart were not ill suited to his lofty pretensions. He was in the prime of youth, tall and handsome, of a fair complexion; he had a light-coloured periwig with his own hair combed over the front: he wore the Highland dress, that is, a tartan short coat without the plaid, a blue bonnet on his head, and on his breast the star of St Andrew. . . .

The Highlanders, when they entered the town in the morning, had secured the heralds and pursuivants: at mid-day they surrounded the Cross with a body of armed men, and obliged the heralds to proclaim King James. . . . An immense multitude witnessed this ceremony, which was performed at noon.

HOME

10.
Prince Charles at Holyrood
22 September - 31 October 1745

John Home did not return to Edinburgh until after Prince Charles had left it, but claims that 'the following short account is extracted from the Memoirs of an officer in his army, who saw him every day'.

The Prince Regent in the morning before the council met, had a levee of his officers, and other people who favoured his cause. When the council rose, . . . Charles dined in public with his principal officers. After dinner he rode out with his life guards, and usually went to Duddingston, where his army lay. In the evening he returned to Holyroodhouse, and received the ladies who came to his drawing-room: he then supped in public, and generally there was music, and a ball afterwards.

HOME

11.
The Noblest Prospect
15 November 1762

London, not Edinburgh, was now the Capital. Boswell was one of a great new class of Scots, still numerous and important to this day. They were not popular with the Londoners, who had not forgotten their fright at the prospect of seeing the Jacobites' claymores in action at Finchley, but the Union had opened London's gates to those Scotsmen on the make, and many of them got on very well indeed. Boswell was no fool either, though he sometimes behaved in a peculiar manner.

MONDAY 15 NOVEMBER. Elated with the thoughts of my journey to London, I got up. . . . I had a long serious talk with my father and mother. They were very kind to me. . . . The scene of being a son setting out from home for the wide world and the idea of being my own master, pleased me much. . . .

At ten I got into my chaise, and away I went. As I passed the Cross, the cadies and chairmen bowed and seemed to say, "GOD prosper long our noble Boswell." I rattled down the High Street in high elevation of spirits, bowed and smiled to acquaintances, and took up my partner at Boyd's Close. . . . I made the chaise stop at the foot of the Canongate; . . . walked to the Abbey of Holyroodhouse, went around the piazzas, bowed thrice: once to the Palace itself, once to the crown of Scotland above the gate in front, and once to the venerable old chapel. I next stood in the court before the Palace, and bowed thrice to Arthur Seat, that lofty romantic mountain on which I have so often strayed in the days of my youth, indulged meditation and felt the raptures of a soul filled with ideas of the magnificence of GOD and his creation. Having thus gratified my agreeable whim and superstitious humour, I felt a warm glow of satisfaction. Indeed I have a strong turn to what the cool part of mankind have named superstition. But this proceeds from my genius for poetry, which ascribes many fanciful properties to everything. . . . I am surely much happier in this way than if I just considered Holyroodhouse as so much stone and lime which has been put together in a certain way, and Arthur Seat as so much earth and rock raised above the neighbouring plains. . . .

BOSWELL

12.
The Factious Barbarians of London
23 August 1765

In 1765 David Hume the philosopher was appointed British chargé d'affaires in Paris, where he was highly respected and much loved: but only a few weeks later he was informed that he was soon going to be recalled, and began trying to decide where he should settle down to spend the rest of his life. In 1769 he finally returned to Edinburgh, and here he died in 1776.

. . . I have not determin'd where I shall pass my latter days: This Place [Paris] should be the most agreeable to me; but a man, who came late thither, and who is not supported by Family Connexions, may perhaps find himself misplac'd even in this Center of Letters and good Society. I have a Reluctance to think of living among the factious Barbarians of London, who will hate me because I am a Scotsman & am not a Whig, and despise me because I am a man of Letters. My Attachment to Edinburgh revives, as I turn my Face towards it. . . .

HUME

13.
Dr Johnson's Visit to Edinburgh
14 August 1773

The exact meaning of Dr Johnson's famous remark may give us something to think about, especially the force of the word, 'you'.

Mr. Johnson and I walked arm-in-arm up the High-street to my house in James's Court: it was a dusky night: I could not prevent his being assailed by the evening effluvia of Edinburgh. I heard a late baronet, of some distinction in the political world in the beginning of the present reign, observe, that 'walking the streets of Edinburgh at night was pretty perilous, and a good deal odoriferous.' The peril is much abated, by the care which the magistrates have taken to enforce the city laws against throwing foul water from the windows; but, from the structure of the houses in the old town, which consist of many stories, in each of which a different family lives, and there being no covered sewers, the odour still continues. A zealous Scotsman would have wished Mr. Johnson to be without one of his five senses upon this occasion. As we marched slowly along, he grumbled in my ear, 'I smell you in the dark!' But he acknowledged that the breadth of the street, and the loftiness of the buildings on each side made a noble appearance.

BOSWELL

14.
Auld Reikie
1773

Robert Fergusson, born in Edinburgh of Aberdonian parents, is the town's own poet. His Edinburgh poems are about the place, not about Robert Fergusson. A strong feature of his poetry is that there is so little of himself consciously introduced. Social life in eighteenth-century Edinburgh went on largely away from home, in cosy taverns and clubs and underground dens, where poetry and song were as usual and necessary for a merry evening as the liquor and the pewter pots, and men of powerful minds were not so scarce that a poet should feel strange in their company, or suspect that he was some different kind of being. Fergusson's life was in many ways tragic, but in this respect he was very fortunate. 'Auld Reekie' is an affectionate term for Edinburgh, as London is known as 'The Smoke'.

Now Morn, with bonny Purpie-smiles,
Kisses the Air-cock o' St. Giles;
Rakin their ᵃEin, the Servant Lasses   ᵃ *eyes*
Early begin their Lies and ᵇClashes;   ᵇ *gossip*
Ilk tells her Friend of saddest Distress,
That still she ᶜbrooks frae scouling Mistress;   ᶜ *endures*

And wi' her ^dJoe in Turnpike Stair   ^d *friend*
She's rather snuff the stinking Air,
^eAs be subjected to her Tongue,   ^e *than*
When justly censur'd in the Wrong.

     On Stair wi' TUB, or ^aPAT in hand,   ^a *pot*
The Barefoot HOUSEMAIDS ^blooe to stand,   ^b *love*
That ^cantrin Fock may ken how ^dSNELL   ^c *passers-by*   ^d *keen*
Auld Reikie will at MORNING SMELL:
Then, with an INUNDATION BIG as
The BURN that 'neath the NORE LOCH BRIG is,
They kindly shower EDINA'S Roses,
To QUICKEN and REGALE our NOSES.
Now some for this, wi' ^eSatyr's Leesh,   ^e *satire's licence*
Ha'e gi'en auld Edinburgh a ^fCreesh: ^f *swipe*
But without Souring ^gnocht is sweet;   ^g *nothing*
The Morning smells that hail our Street,
Prepare, and gently lead the Way
To ^hSimmer ⁱcanty, braw and gay: ^h *summer*   ⁱ *cheerful*
Edina's Sons ^jmair eithly share   ^j *more easily*
Her Spices and her Dainties rare,
^kThen he that's never yet been call'd   ^k *than*
^lAff frae his Plaidie or his ^mFauld. . . .   ^l *off*   ^m *fold*

FRAE joyous Tavern, reeling drunk,
Wi' fiery Phizz, and ^aEin half sunk,   ^a *eyes*
^bBehad the Bruiser, ^cFae to a'   ^b *behold*   ^c *foe*
That in the reek o' ^dGardies fa':   ^d *garbage*
Close by his Side, a ^efeckless Race   ^e *feeble, worthless*
O' Macaronies shew their Face,
And think they're free frae Skaith or Harm,
While Pith befriends their Leaders Arm:
Yet fearfu' ^faften o' their ^gMaught,   ^f *often*   ^g *might*
They quatt the Glory o' the ^hFaught   ^h *fight*
To this same Warriour wha led
ⁱThae Heroes to bright Honour's Bed;   ⁱ *those*
And aft the hack o' Honour shines
In Bruiser's Face wi' broken Lines:
Of them sad Tales he tells anon,
Whan Ramble and whan Fighting's done;
And, like Hectorian, ne'er impairs
The Brag and Glory o' his ^jSairs.   ^j *hurts*

     WHAN Feet in dirty Gutters plash,
And ^aFock to ^bwale their Fitstaps ^cfash;   ^a *folk*   ^b *choose*   ^c *fuss*
At night the Macaroni drunk
In Pools or Gutters ^daftimes sunk: ^d *oft-times*
Hegh! what a Fright he now appears,
Whan he his Corpse dejected rears!
Look at that Head, and think if there
The ^ePomet ^fslaister'd up his Hair!   ^e *pomatum*   ^f *plastered*
The Cheeks observe, where now cou'd shine
The ^gscancing Glories o' Carmine?   ^g *shining*
Ah, Legs! in vain the Silk-worm there
Display'd to View her ^heidant Care;   ^h *diligent*
For Stink, instead of Perfumes, grow,
And ⁱclarty Odours fragrant flow. . . .   ⁱ *filthy*

182

ON Sunday here, an alter'd Scene
O' Men and Manners meets our ^aEin: *^a eyes*
Ane wad ^bmaist ^ctrow some People chose   *^b almost   ^c believe*
To change their Faces wi' their Clo'es,
And ^dfain wad ^egar ^filk Neighbour think   *^d gladly   ^e make   ^f each*
They thirst for Goodness, as for Drink:
But there's an ^gunco Dearth o' Grace,   *^g remarkable*
That has nae Mansion but the Face,
And never can obtain a Part
In ^hbenmost Corner of the Heart.   *^h innermost*
Why should Religion make us sad,
If good frae Virtue's to be had?
Na, rather gleefu' turn your Face;
Forsake Hypocrisy, Grimace;
And never have it understood
You ⁱfleg Mankind frae being good.   *ⁱ frighten*
    IN Afternoon, a' ^abrawly buskit,   *^a dressed in their best*
The Joes and Lasses ^bloe to frisk it: *^b love*
Some tak a great delight to place
The modest ^cBongrace o'er the Face;   *^c large straw bonnet*
Tho' you may see, if so inclin'd,
The turning o' the Leg behind.
Now Comely-Garden, and the Park,
Refresh them, after Forenoon's ^dwark;   *^d work*
Newhaven, Leith or Canon-mills,
Supply them in their Sunday's Gills;
Whare ^eWriters aften spend their Pence,   *^e solicitors*
To stock their Heads wi' Drink and Sense.

              FERGUSSON

Top Living
1773

15.

There are no oysters in these waters now, but there must be several square miles of mussels, complete with notice-boards warning you not to eat them. However, a certain amount of fishing still goes on in the Firth.

Of a' the waters that can ^ahobble   *^a toss*
A fishin ^byole or salmon coble,   *^b yawl*
And can reward the fishers' trouble,
    Or south or north,
There's ^cnane sae spacious and sae noble   *^c none*
    As Firth O' *Forth*.

In her the skate and codlin sail,
The ^aeil ^bfou souple wags her tail,   *^a eel   ^b full*
Wi' herrin, ^cfleuk, and mackarel,   *^c flounder*
    And ^dwhitens daily: *^d whitings*
Their spindle-shanks the labsters trail,
    Wi' ^epartans plenty.   *^e crabs*

AULD REIKIE'S sons blyth faces wear;
September's merry month is near,
That brings in Neptune's *caller chere,   *a* *fresh*
    New oysters fresh;
The halesomest and nicest *b*gear   *b* *supply*
    Of fish or flesh. . . .

Whan big as burns the gutters *a*rin,   *a* *run*
*b*Gin ye hae catcht a *c*droukit skin,   *b* *if*   *c* *soaked*
To *Luckie Middlemist*'s *d*loup in,   *d* *leap*
    And sit fu snug
O'er oysters and a dram o' gin,
    Or haddock *e*lug.   *e* lit. *ear*

When auld Saunct Giles, at *a*aught o'clock,   *a* *eight*
*b*Gars merchant *c*lowns their *d*chopies lock,   *b* *makes*   *c* *fellows*   *d* *booths*
There we adjourn wi' hearty *e*fock   *e* *folk*
    To *f*birle our bodles   *f* *spend our money*
And get wharewi' to crack our joke,
    And clear our noddles. . . .

At *Musselbrough*, and eke *Newhaven*,
The fisher-wives will get *top livin*,
Whan lads *a*gang out on *b*Sunday's even   *a* *go*   *b* *Saturday night*
    To treat their *c*joes,   *c* *girl-friends*
And tak of fat *d*pandours a *e*prieven,   *d* *large oysters*   *e* *taste*
    Or *mussel-*f*brose*. . . .   *f* *broth*

FERGUSSON

16.   Enbrugh Gentry
1787

Burns always acknowledged how much he owed to his predecessors Allan Ramsay the poet,
Hamilton of Gilbertfield, and especially Robert Fergusson; and there is no need to make any
editorial comment on the rebuke that he addressed to the gentry of Edinburgh.

. . . My senses wad be in a *a*creel,   *a* lit. *basket*
Should I but dare a *hope* to *b*speel,   *b* *climb*
Wi' *Allan*, or wi' *Gilbertfield*,
    The *c*braes o' fame;   *c* *hillsides*
Or Ferguson, the *d*writer-chiel,   *d* *lawyer-fellow*
    A deathless name.

O *Ferguson*! Thy glorious parts
Ill suited law's dry, musty arts!
My curse upon your *a*whunstane hearts,   *a* *whinstone*
    Ye Enbrugh Gentry!
The *b*tythe o' what ye waste at *c*cartes   *b* *tenth*   *c* *cards*
    *d*Wad stow'd his pantry! . . .   *d* *would have stocked*

BURNS

17

The Bad Old Days
1799

Ever since the mid-nineteenth century, Edinburgh has enjoyed a much higher standard of municipal government than in the bad old days before the passing of the Reform Bill in 1832. In the late eighteenth century, Henry Dundas, Viscount Melville, Pitt's proconsul in Scotland, wielded so much official patronage that he was called 'Henry IX'; and, according to Lord Cockburn, all sorts of abuses flourished.

The Council Chamber ... was a low-roofed room, very dark, and very dirty, with some small dens off it for clerks.

Within this Pandemonium sat the town-council, omnipotent, corrupt, impenetrable. Nothing was beyond its grasp; no variety of opinion disturbed its unanimity, for the pleasure of Dundas was the sole rule for every one of them. ... Silent, powerful, submissive, mysterious, and irresponsible, they might have been sitting in Venice. Certain of the support of the Proconsul, whom they no more thought of thwarting than of thwarting Providence, timidity was not one of their vices. About the year 1799 a solitary schism amazed the public, by disclosing the incredible fact that the town-council might contain a member who had an opinion of his own. A councillor, named Smith, electrified the city by a pamphlet showing that the city was bankrupt. Time has put it beyond all doubt that he was right; and fortunate would it have been for the city and its creditors if this had been acknowledged at the time, instead of being aggravated by years of subsequent extravagance and concealment.

COCKBURN

18

The Honours of Scotland
5 February 1818

Robert the Bruce's crown, closed with four arches by order of James V, the Sceptre, with the initials of James V, and the Sword, presented by Pope Julius to James IV in 1507, are the three main objects that constitute the Honours of Scotland. The story of their preservation, through many dangers in times of defeat and occupation, and of the mysterious oak chest deposited in the Castle in 1707, discovered in the windowless room in 1794, thought to be empty because it sounded so when shaken, and opened on the occasion here described by Lockhart, reads like an imaginative tale of adventure.

John Gibson Lockhart, described on the wall of his house at 25 Northumberland Street as 'son in law and biographer of Sir Walter Scott', did in fact shine with a light of his own, contributing to Blackwood's Magazine and editing the Quarterly Review, as well as writing the admirable Biography.

On the 5th ..., Scott and several of his brother Commissioners revisited the Castle, accompanied by some of the ladies of their families. His daughter tells me that her father's conversation had worked her feelings up to such a pitch, that when the lid was again removed, she nearly fainted, and drew back from the circle. As she was retiring, she was startled by his voice exclaiming, in a tone of the deepest emotion, 'something between anger and despair,' as she expresses it—'G— NO!' One of the Commissioners, not quite entering into the solemnity with which Scott regarded this business, had, it seems, made a sort of motion as if he meant to put the crown on the head of one of the young ladies near him, but the voice and aspect of the Poet were more than sufficient to make the worthy gentleman understand his error; and respecting the enthusiasm with which he had not been taught to sympathize, he laid down the ancient diadem with an air of painful embarrassment. Scott whispered, 'Pray forgive me;' and turning round at the moment, observed his daughter deadly pale, and leaning by the door. He immediately drew her out of the room, and when the air had somewhat recovered her, walked with her across the Mound to Castle Street. 'He never spoke all the way home,' she says, 'but every now and then, I felt his arm tremble; and from that time I fancied he began to treat me more like a woman than a child. I thought he liked me better, too, than he had ever done before.'

These little incidents may give some notion of the profound seriousness with which his imagination had invested this matter. I am obliged to add, that in the society of Edinburgh at the time, even in the highest Tory circles, it did not seem to awaken much even of curiosity—to say nothing of any deeper feeling; there was, however, a great excitement among the common people of the town, and a still greater among the peasantry, not only in the neighbourhood, but all over Scotland; and the Crown-room, becoming thenceforth one of the established *lions* of a city much resorted to, moreover, by stranger tourists, was likely, on the most moderate scale of admission-fee, to supply a revenue sufficient for remunerating responsible and respectable guardianship.

LOCKHART

19.   Edinburgh Mon Amour
c. 1820

In course of his detailed disquisition on love, Stendhal studies a department of life somewhat neglected by the Edinburgh annalists. Even in the presence of ladies, the gentlemen would apparently prefer to discuss the less romantic branches of Natural Philosophy. Thanks largely to James Hutton's pioneering studies of Salisbury Crags and Arthur's Seat, where old sandstone is exposed beneath igneous rock, geology was then beginning to be an exact science; and although Stendhal found the controversy between the Neptunians and Vulcanians so boring a subject of conversation, 'Hutton's section' is still of interest to geologists from all over the world.

One cannot be unaware of the underlying melancholy with which Scottish women are endowed. This melancholy is seen at its most fascinating in the ballroom, where it imparts a unique relish to the ardent alacrity with which they leap in performing their national dances. Another advantage which Edinburgh possesses is that of having emancipated itself from the mean omnipotence of gold; and in that respect (no less than in the singular and savage beauty of its situation) it presents a complete contrast with London. Like Rome, the beautiful city of Edinburgh seems rather to be a proper retreat for the life of contemplation. The restless vortex, the agitating concerns of the life of action, with all its advantages and inconveniences, belong to London. Edinburgh seems to me to pay its forfeit to the Evil One by being a little inclined to pedantry. The times when Mary Stuart inhabited the ancient Abbey of Holyrood, and when Rizzio was assassinated in her arms, were richer in love (all women will acknowledge it) than those in which it is disputed, so interminably, and even in their presence, what preference should be accorded to the Neptunian or Vulcanian system of $X, Y, Z \ldots$

I shall say nothing about the terrible Scottish Sunday, in comparison with which London's resembles a pleasure-party. This day designed to honour Heaven is the best image of Hell that I have ever seen on Earth. 'Let's not go so fast', said a Scotsman to a French friend of his, while returning from church; 'people might think we were just taking a walk.'

STENDHAL

20.   Mine Own Romantic Town
c. 1878

Central Edinburgh is still very much a contrast between the Old Town and the New Town, from Princes Street northwards. Stevenson was born in New Town respectability to a family that had won success by building lighthouses and other great works, and stayed in Heriot Row, but to him the Old Town was a place of wonder.

In almost every one of Stevenson's Edinburgh essays, you find washings hanging out somewhere. In our day, as in his, the New Town washings do not catch the eye; they are not seen in Abercromby Place or Nelson Street (except round the back): but in the Old Town they may still add a patch of whiter-than-white, even to the Canongate Churchyard or to Tweeddale Court.

The peculiar effect of light that Stevenson noticed is perhaps most wonderful when a low sun, out of an otherwise dark sky, brings out the light of the stone, and flashes from the old uneven glass.

Again, meditative people will find a charm in a certain consonancy between the aspect of the city and its odd and stirring history. Few places, if any, offer a more barbaric display of contrasts to the eye. In the very midst stands one of the most satisfactory crags in Nature —a Bass Rock upon dry land rooted in a garden, shaken by passing trains, carrying a crown of battlements and turrets, and describing its warlike shadow over the liveliest and brightest thoroughfare of the new town. From their smoky beehives, ten stories high, the unwashed look down upon the open squares and gardens of the wealthy; and gay people sunning themselves along Princes Street, with its mile of commercial palaces all beflagged upon some great occasion, see, across a gardened valley set with statues, where the washings of the old town flutter in the breeze at its high windows. And then, upon all sides, what a clashing of architecture! In this one valley, where the life of the town goes most busily forward, there may be seen, shown one above and behind another by the accidents of the ground, buildings in almost every style upon the globe. Egyptian and Greek temples, Venetian palaces and Gothic spires, are huddled one over another in a most admired disorder; while, above all, the brute mass of the Castle and the summit of Arthur's Seat look down upon these imitations with a becoming dignity, as the works of Nature may look down upon the monuments of Art. But Nature is a more indiscriminate patroness than we imagine, and in no way frightened of a strong effect. The birds roost as willingly among the Corinthian capitals as in the crannies of the crag; the same atmosphere and daylight clothe the eternal rock and yesterday's imitation portico; and as the soft northern sunshine throws out everything into a glorified distinctness—or easterly mists, coming up with the blue evening, fuse all these incongruous features into one, and the lamps begin to glitter along the street, and faint lights to burn in the high windows across the valley—the feeling grows upon you that this also is a piece of Nature in the most intimate sense; that this profusion of eccentricities, this dream in masonry and living rock is not a dropscene in a theatre, but a city in the world of everyday reality, connected by railway and telegraph-wire with all the capitals of Europe, and inhabited by citizens of the familiar type, who keep ledgers, and attend church, and have sold their immortal portion to a daily paper. By all the canons of romance, the place demands to be half-deserted and leaning towards decay; birds we might admit in profusion, the play of the sun and winds, and a few gypsies encamped in the chief thoroughfare; but these citizens, with their cabs and tramways, their trains and posters, are altogether out of key. Chartered tourists, they make free with historic localities, and rear their young among the most picturesque sites with a grand human indifference. To see them thronging by, in their neat clothes and conscious moral rectitude, and with a little air of possession that verges on the absurd, is not the least striking feature of the place.*

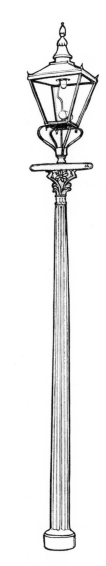

One of Edinburgh's elegant old lamposts.

STEVENSON

* These sentences have, I fear, given offence in my native town, and a proportionable pleasure to our rivals of Glasgow. . . . To the Glasgow people I would say only one word, and that is of gold: *I have not yet written a book about Glasgow.*

187

21.   From the South Seas
                              1894

Even in the midst of the Pacific, a few weeks before he died, Stevenson still remembered
Edinburgh as vividly as ever.

> . . . Hearkening I heard afar
> In my precipitous city beaten bells
> Winnow the keen sea wind. . . .
>   STEVENSON

22.   Wind in the Crescent
                              1948

In a lively little poem, the Italian poet Eugenio Montale records some of the impressions that
Edinburgh made on him in 1948.

> Il grande ponte non portava a te.
> T' avrei raggiunta anche navigando
> nelle chiaviche, a un tuo comando. Ma
> già le forze, col sole sui cristalli
> Delle verande, andavano stremandosi.
>
> L'uomo che predicava sul Crescente
> mi chiese « Sai dov'è Dio? » Lo sapevo
> e glielo dissi. Scosse il capo. Sparve
> nel turbine che prese uomini e case
> e li sollevò in alto, sulla pece.

Edimburgo. 1948*   MONTALE

 * [The big bridge didn't lead to you. I'd have reached you even by navigating the sewers, if
you'd uttered one word of command. But already my strength, with the sun on the glass of the
verandahs, was beginning to fail.
  [The man who was preaching on the Crescent asked me 'Do you know where God is?' I knew,
and told him. He shook his head, disappeared, in the whirlwind which seized people and houses
and lifted them high up on pitch-blackness.—Edinburgh 1948.]

23.   Embro tae the Ploy
                             c. 1950

In 'Embro tae the Ploy', a sardonic commentary on life in Edinburgh during the Festival which
Robert Garioch modelled on a medieval Scots poem called 'Peblis to the Play', Fergusson
would surely have recognised the work of a kindred spirit.

In simmer, whan aa sorts forgether
In Embro tae the Ploy,
Folk seek out *a*friens tae hae a blether   *a friends*
Or faes they'd fain annoy.
*b*Smorit wi British Railways' *c*reek   *b smothered   c smoke*
Frae Glesca or Glen Roy
Or Wick they come tae hae a week
O cultivated joy
                    Or three
At Embro tae the Ploy.

Americans wi *a*routh o dollars   *a plenty*
'at drinks our whisky neat,
Wi Sassenachs an' Oxford scholars
Are *b*eydent for the treat   *b diligent*
O music sedulously high-tie
At thirty bob a seat:
Wop opera performed in Eyetie
Tae them's richt up their street,
                    They say,
At Embro tae the Ploy . . . .

The Café Royal an' Abbotsford
Are filled wi *a*orra folk   *a extraordinary*
Wha's stock-in-trade's the *b*scrievit word   *b written*
Or twicet-scrievit joke.
Brains, weak or strang, in heavy beer,
Or ordinary, soak.
*e*Quo ane, 'This *d*yill is awfie dear,   *e quoth one   d ale*
I hae nae *g*clinks in *f*poke,   *g coins   f pocket*
                    Nor foldin-money
At Embro tae the Ploy.'

The auld Assembly Rooms, whaur Scott
Forgethert wi' his *a*fiers,   *a cronies*
Nou see a *b*gey kenspeckle lot   *b very conspicuous*
*c*Ablow the chandeliers.   *c beneath*
Tae Embro *d*drouths, the festive club   *d thirsts*
A richt Godsend appears;
It's something new tae find a pub
That gangs on servin beers
                    Fu late
At Embro tae the Ploy.

They toddle hame doun mirky streets,
Filled wi synthetic joy;
A-weel, the year brings few *a*sic treats   *a such*
An' *b*muckle tae annoy.   *b much*
There's mony hartsome braw hy-jinks
Mixed up in this alloy
In simmer whan aa sorts forgether
In Embro tae the Ploy.

                    GARIOCH

189

24. # Vox Populi
1963

Garioch says that he overheard some of this dialogue between two interested Edinburgh citizens in Princes Street during King Olav's state visit.

Whu's aw thae fflag-poles ffur in Princes Street?
Chwoich! Ptt! Hechyuch! Ab-boannie ccairy-on,
seez-owre the wa'er, whu' the deevil's thon
in aidie, heh?—The Queen's t'meet

the King o' Norway wi his royal suite.—
His royal whu'?—The hale jing-bang, it's aw in
the papur, whaur's ma speck-sh? Aye, we're gaun
t'hing the flags up. Mind whan we got beat

in Norway? Ye're no lisnun whu' A say,
A tellt ye thaim an us wad aye be mates,
weill, A wuz richt, an nou we're gaun t'hae

a wee-bit celebration on the Rates.—
Ahd-dae-ken whu' the place is ccomin tae,
wi aw thae, hechyuch! fforeign po'entates.

GARIOCH

25. # Auld Reekie
1963

In this deceptively simple little poem, Sydney Goodsir Smith, another modern Scottish poet whose best work often recalls Fergusson's, catches another of Edinburgh's many moods.

Like a great beast sleepin sound
Auld Reekie ^aliggs   ^a *lies*
^bCauld in its enchantment   ^b *cold*
Its cage ^cbleezin wi licht   ^c *blazing*
For passing wonderment.

But look, the auld dream
^aBirsles its hairy coat   ^a *bristles*
It ^bsteers in its sleep   ^b *stirs*
Lurches blind against the bars—
Let me out! Let me out!
I want life in my grip.

GOODSIR SMITH

REFERENCES

In all items marked *, the original spelling and punctuation have been slightly modified.

1. John Barbour, *The Bruce*, ed. W. M. Mackenzie, London, 1909, x. 606 ff.

2. William Dunbar, *'We that ar Heir in Hevins Glory', in *The Poems of William Dunbar*, ed. W. M. Mackenzie, Edinburgh 1932, pp. 56 ff.

3. *Extracts from the Records of the Burgh of Edinburgh A.D. 1403-1528*, Edinburgh 1869, pp. 143 ff.

4. Translated from Pierre de Bourdeilles, Abbé de Brantôme, *Vies des femmes illustres*, ed. L. Moland, nouvelle édition, Paris n.d., pp. 117 f.

5. *'A Breefe and True Relatione of the Broyle which fell out on the Lords Day, the 23rd of July, 1637. . . .', printed in John, Earl of Rothes, *A Relation of the Proceedings concerning the Affairs of the Kirk of Scotland*, Edinburgh (Bannatyne Club) 1830, pp. 198 f.

6. *'A Note of the several Passages concerning Montrose his Carriage after he was Broght Prisoner to Edinburgh', in the Miscellany of the Maitland Club, Vol. II (*Royal Letters and Instructions, and other Documents, from the Archives of the Earls of Wigton MDXX-MDCL*), Edinburgh 1840, pp. 482 ff.

7. Daniel Defoe, *The History of the Union of Great Britain*, Edinburgh 1709: 'Of the Carrying On of the Treaty in Scotland', pp. 27 ff.

8. *Council Record* (25 May to 21 Dec. 1737), pp. 137 f.

9, 10. John Home, *The History of the Rebellion in the Year 1745*, in *The Works of John Home, Esq.*, Edinburgh 1822, pp. 66 ff., 116.

11. James Boswell, *London Journal 1762-1763*, ed. F. A. Pottle, London 1950, pp. 40 ff.

12. David Hume, letter to Rev. Hugh Blair, dated Paris 25 Aug. 1765, in *Letters of David Hume*, ed. J. Y. T. Greig, Oxford 1932, I.517.

13. James Boswell, *Journal of a Tour to the Hebrides*, ed. R. W. Chapman, London 1934, p. 173.

14. Robert Fergusson, 'Auld Reikie, A Poem', in *The Poems of Robert Fergusson*, ed. M. P. McDiarmid, Scottish Text Society, Vol. II, Edinburgh 1956, pp. 109 ff.

15. Robert Fergusson, 'Caller Oysters', *op. cit.*, pp. 66 ff.

16. Robert Burns, *'To William Simpson, Ochiltree', in *Poems, chiefly in the Scottish Dialect*, Edinburgh 1787, p. 292.

17. Henry Cockburn, *Memorials of his Time*, Edinburgh 1856, pp. 94 f.

18. John Gibson Lockhart, *Memoirs of the Life of Sir Walter Scott, Bart*, London 1837, IV. 118 f.

19. Translated from Stendhal, *De l'Amour*, ed. H. Martineau, Paris (Cluny) 1938, pp. 181 f.

20. Robert Louis Stevenson, *Edinburgh: Picturesque Notes* (1879), in *The Works of Robert Louis Stevenson*, Skerryvore Edition, XXVI (1925), pp. 6 f.

21. Robert Louis Stevenson, dedication 'To My Wife', in *Weir of Hermiston*, London 1896, p. v.

22. Eugenio Montale, 'Vento sulla Mezzaluna', in *Poesie III*, Milan (Mondadori) 1957, p. 51.

23, 24. Robert Garioch, *'Embro tae the Ploy', in *Scottish Verse 1851-1951*, ed. D. C. C. Young, Edinburgh 1952, pp. 253 ff., and 'Six Edinburgh Sonnets', in *Lines Review*, 19 (Winter 1963), p. 7.

25. Sydney Goodsir Smith, 'Auld Reekie 1963', in *Scotland's Magazine*, LIX (Jan. 1963), p. 43.

Endpapers. The views reproduced in the endpapers include two overlapping sections of the 'Prospect of Edinburgh from the North', one of the engravings included in G. Slezer's *Theatrum Scotiae* (1719).

Line-Drawings. The line-drawings reproduced on pp. 3, 165, 187, and 192 were specially made for this book by J. Brian Crossland.

A medieval carving of the escutcheon in the City's coat of arms.